C000052257

THE FUTURE OF WORK

The future of work is a vital contemporary area of debate both in business and management research, and in wider social, political and economic discourse. Globally relevant issues, including the ageing workforce, rise of the gig economy, workplace automation and changing forms of business ownership, are all regularly the subject of discussion in both academic research and the mainstream media, having wider professional and public policy implications.

The Future of Work series features books examining key issues or challenges in the modern workplace, synthesising prior developments in critical thinking, alongside current practical challenges in order to interrogate possible future developments in the world of work.

Offering future research agendas and suggesting practical outcomes for today's and tomorrow's businesses and workforce, the books in this series a present powerful, challenging and polemical analysis of a diverse range of subjects in their potential to address future challenges and possible new trajectories.

The series highlights what changes still need to be made to core areas of business practice and theory in order for them to be forward facing, more representative and able to fulfil the industrial challenges of the future.

Forthcoming Titles

Algorithms, Blockchain & Cryptocurrency: Implications for the Future of the Workplace
Gavin Brown and Richard Whittle

Workforce Health and Productivity
Stephen Bevan and Cary L. Cooper

Spending Without Thinking: The Future of Consumption
Richard Whittle

Personnel Selection: Finding the Future of Talent through Science and Technology
Tomas Chamorro-Premuzic, Franziska Leutner and Reece Akhtar

Cooperatives at Work
George Cheney, Matt Noyes and Emi Do

CAREERS: THINKING, STRATEGISING AND PROTOTYPING

ANN M. BREWER
University of Newcastle, Australia

United Kingdom – North America – Japan – India
Malaysia – China

Emerald Publishing Limited
Howard House, Wagon Lane, Bingley BD16 1WA, UK

First edition 2020

Copyright © 2020 Emerald Publishing Limited

Reprints and permissions service
Contact: permissions@emeraldinsight.com

No part of this book may be reproduced, stored in a retrieval
system, transmitted in any form or by any means electronic,
mechanical, photocopying, recording or otherwise without
either the prior written permission of the publisher or a licence
permitting restricted copying issued in the UK by The Copyright
Licensing Agency and in the USA by The Copyright Clearance
Center. No responsibility is accepted for the accuracy of
information contained in the text, illustrations or advertisements.
The opinions expressed in these chapters are not necessarily
those of the Author or the publisher.

British Library Cataloguing in Publication Data
A catalogue record for this book is available from the British
Library

ISBN: 978-1-83867-210-2 (Print)
ISBN: 978-1-83867-207-2 (Online)
ISBN: 978-1-83867-209-6 (Epub)

ISOQAR certified
Management System,
awarded to Emerald
for adherence to
Environmental
standard
ISO 14001:2004.

Certificate Number 1985
ISO 14001

INVESTOR IN PEOPLE

To my son, remembering the places we went ...

Navigating and nurturing a career is one of the most critical personal and organisational challenges of our time. Here Professor Brewer tackles the issues with insight, intellect and integrity recognising the evolving context of work, skills and fulfilment. *Careers* provides valuable tools and frameworks for the workforce planner, policy maker and business leader. Significantly, it highlights the imperative for a human centric approach, drawing a distinct and positive parallel between successful career making and city shaping.

Katherine O'Regan
Executive Director
Sydney Business Chamber

CONTENTS

PART II: STRATEGISING CAREERS

PART III: PROTOTYPING CAREERS

LIST OF FIGURES AND TABLES

PART I

THINKING CAREERS

1

WHAT IS A CAREER IN THE 21ST CENTURY?

INTRODUCTION

Careers single out lives and shape them in profound ways. The notion of a career is not a straightforward concept and, increasingly, it has become more complicated. Many young people today will have multiple careers in diverse industries.

The aim, in writing this book, is to delve into the concept of career to understand how people consider their careers to understand the totality of what is at stake. As we think about the next 50 years of career making, we are only too aware of how unpredictable work and careers are becoming as new industries and divisions of labour are rapidly spawned. One must consider the possibility of different career trajectories in the face of globalisation's tendency to homogenise; and recognise the multiple coexisting meanings that embody career.

The mutable nature of work means it is time to take a fresh look at what is meant by the term career and career pathway. An increasing number of people are working in jobs that do not require either their skills or credentials. Like Robert

Frost[1], people ponder which road to take – the one more often chosen, the one less travelled or the one yet to be discovered.

Careers contain meaning, processes, collections of diverse stories and practices that are neither stagnant nor do they have fixed boundaries. The meanings, emotions and bonds that individuals and groups acquire are important in the diverse operationalisation of career.

Careers are 'spaces' becoming meaningful over time. People establish strong bonds and emotions within their careers leading to a sense of attachment, identity and dependence. A career attachment is either strong or weak. In many cases, people become career dependent and rely on a particular role to suit their individual needs and desires, which is often unrecognised or acknowledged until the point of a career transition such as redundancy or retirement.

A career signifies a particular, bounded function with skills, knowledge and attributes attached. It is a way of seeing, knowing and understanding the world; hence, careers mean different things to different people. For example, a career is considered as a meaningful pursuit entailing goals and outcomes rather than defined by fixed role specifications. This process allows people with careers to develop social relationships as well as the emotional and subjective bonds with others; opportunities often denied to those who are unemployed.

Generally speaking, people searching for a career are looking for a long-term commitment and identity – that is, continuity of engagement and benefits. For people with careers in the past and now, they offer people a purpose for their life as well as a chance for becoming something beyond themselves as well as membership in a select group. This membership leads to a heightened sense of identity and meaning for the incumbent.

Career Stakeholders

As shown in Fig. 1, embarking on, developing and sustaining a career is more often than not, dependent on various stakeholders and their level of investment and commitment, directly or indirectly, in a person's pathway. The extent and nature of the stakeholders' engagement with a specific career incumbent is considerable from supervision through to a vested interest in the outcome.

The period of stakeholder engagement varies for each type of connection as does the degree of engagement with the incumbent or their overall investment in the career stakeholding. Fig. 1 also depicts the career incumbent's family as a crucial and highly engaged stakeholder, although despite goodwill is not always guiding in the best interests of the incumbent. Any specific stakeholder's influence is multidimensional, and the degree of their influence varies over time. As the career incumbent establishes their independent status,

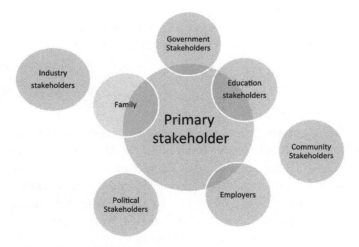

Fig. 1. Career Stakeholders.

their family's influence on their career weakens unless they are the employer.

The understanding of the term career is much wider than in the past to embrace a more comprehensive and multilateral view. As the relationship between employer and employee expands (Rousseau, 1995), conventional employment changes from full-time, casual, contingent or contract-based. These changes are employer driven and adopted eventually by industry and government industries. Employers as invested stakeholders determine the nature and duration of the employment contract. They also control career tracks within their organisations, for example, resources and remuneration. A supervisor as another stakeholder controls the work to be performed. Government, community and political stakeholders influence and are influenced by career outcomes and changes. In some cases, this array of stakeholders has a generalised responsibility for sustaining the work that the primary stakeholder conducts. Other stakeholders shaping careers include customers, clients, students, community members and patients.

Work is purposive for all stakeholders, and career is particularly purposive for the incumbent stakeholder.

Careers and Work

Work, as distinct from career, relates to a specific set of tasks. It depicts the relationship between individual effort and performance in executing these tasks. While work is embedded in the notion of career, the latter takes a wide angle view to include a vocational focus as well as a continuation in maintaining and progressing through particular career track overtime.

Increasing labour market competition and rapid technological change are shaping expectations about careers and work employment. Technological change leads to new opportunities and outcomes for all career stakeholders, while it closes down options for others due to its entry barriers and requirements to maintain membership. Employers require greater mobility and flexibility from employees (Gubler, Arnold, & Coombs, 2014; McMahon, Watson, & Lee, 2019) as business needs change, which impacts on careers and so career change is less remarkable than it once was. At any given point, a person is either in a career, in the midst of a career transition, for example, embarking on a career for the first time, or transitioning to retirement.

The backdrop in this book is the changing nature of industrially developed societies in which having a career is celebrated and equated with success. In many societies, careers remain protected through upholding entry requirements and quotas. Investment in a career is based on a credentialed qualification, which, in the past, was relatively cost-effective as it usually guaranteed employment compared to today. In the past, employment security was relatively assured, as was the prospective return on investment or ROI being comparatively high. Careers were professionally specified by educational, professional or industrial associations, each with their norms and customs that changed overtime progressively. Hyper-specialisation shaped careers in the twentieth century. Hence, there was an aura or 'halo-effect' encircling the notion of a career that transmogrifies it from the mundane to something beyond the ordinary (Gell, 1992). These aspects of careers are changing today.

Career Perspectives, Context and Structures

In this section, careers and career thinking are considered from various, interrelated perspectives: sociological, vocational and psychological. The sociological literature is

focussed on labour market trends and participation and how
work is organised. Questions such as how do labour markets
and organisations change over time, why and what will this
mean for the future, thrive throughout the decades.

Career paths are based on regulatory processes as well as
culture, values and stories (Moore, Gunz, & Hall, 2007; Patton & McIlveen, 2009). These stories are told and retold to
new recruits by others and provide both meaning and support to help people make sense of their world of work. A
vocational approach focusses on the notions of a 'calling',
apprenticeships and occupational skills whereas career paths
and mentorship, an age-old tradition, is making a comeback
in the twenty-first century. Although career meanings vary,
there are several factors common to most definitions such as
the arrangement of positions, attitudes, actions that a person experiences in employment (Arnold & Jackson, 1997;
Greenhaus, Callanan, & Godschalk, 2010; Hall, 2002;
Khapova & Arthur 2011). Other definitions focus on career
pathways and passages.

A career is an undertaking within a specific context. The
context is differentiated by social, economic and quantifiable
resources, organised for an array of careers, a scope of work
activities of designated requirements, within limits to attain
value for primary, secondary and tertiary stakeholders (based
on Turner, 2014).

The reality of the world of work as people enter it, often
means that what a career provides for and requires of them is
very different from their expectations. Most people who have
been in the workforce for a long time will observe how this
pattern has changed from the time of their first job to their
current one.

Acquiring a career is a complex process, whether starting up a business, helping others or contributing to nation-
building. What contributes to this complexity are the career

aspirations that people hold, sometimes leading to a tension between self-interest (manifested by recognition and acknowledgement by others) and altruism (demonstrated by social responsibility and community engagement). Career choices are triggered at various points in a person's life either from childhood, graduation or even later, in mid-career or at any time in between.

Perceptions of self and identity, both felt and ascribed, will change over their life course too, and this influences career choices. At various times, people encounter situations which lead them to consider changing careers. These career catalysts also vary depending on whether it is finding a new or different challenge, fleeing a demanding supervisor, a toxic workplace culture, a partner moving jobs, through a divorce and so on. Career change activates a process of search, discovery and transition, which this book aims to explore in Chapters 2–6.

In the past, people followed a fairly conservative career trajectory as organisations and households were relatively stable and secure. In those days, a career was considered, if not for life-long, long-term with the promise of longstanding success. Today, organisations and workplaces are in endless fluidity and provide little certainty coupled with declining loyalty between employers and employees, tenure rates and more flexible work alongside changing technology mean that work and hence careers have changed and will continue to do so. Keeping pace with skill development to meet workplace changes is only one part of the equation. As routine skills and jobs are replaced by technology, the demands for capability has shifted from the routine to sophisticated skillsets requiring new thinking. While people in the past could acquire work on experience alone, this is rarely the case today.

Consequently these days, life and career pathways are as diverse and increasingly short-lived. The increasing unpredictability of work suggests that becoming attached and fixed on careers, roles or specific work activities may not be in any one's interests (Vondracek & Porfeli, 2011). Being adaptable and resilient to career changes, letdowns and the like is meaningful.

Career fulfilment depends on continuous skill development, growth and preparation. On balance, work is no longer a task or an activity to be performed within certain hours. Work is an experience that is sought for its intrinsic (e.g. rewarding, autonomous, creative) as much as its extrinsic attributes (e.g. remuneration, location). For example, as Cohen (2013, p. 459) claims jobs

> ... enclosed the people who performed and managed them, the competencies and experiences of those actors, technology, formal and informal rewards, locations in a status hierarchy, human resources policies, bureaucratic rules and regulations, as well as the various requirements that each of these elements produced.

This book picks up all these diverse career aspects. The assumption is that these various factors that people need to deal with as they affect career performance and outcomes. Focussing on why and how individuals and groups progress and cope throughout their working lives, and in what way it manifests itself in people's lives such that their identity is infused by their career achievements and outcomes.

THEMES IN CAREER THINKING

Despite the career complexity outlined above, there are some prominent themes common to career including the context in which the career happens; a career en actor who 'has' the career and experiences it, and the time over which the career takes place (see Collin's, 2007 'time, social space, and the individual'). Careers are structured according to their entry requirements, prescribed steps for progressing careers, their status and changing contexts which are outlined in Chapter 5.

For most people, a career is an umbrella term encompassing all that happens to them as they proceed through life. People will experience 'career-mindedness', that is, 'putting career first in their lives' for example, which is heightened at different times of their life. While career means different things to different people, the universal thread is the striving to achieve something beyond what they have at present, for example, promotion, remuneration or a calling. The career journey will vary for each person as will the markers that set out such a life, for example, employability and retirement. Up to a few decades ago, employers controlled the career paths of individuals. Today, career paths are in the hands of the individual (McDonald & Hite, 2008).

For employed people, most invest the largest part of their life 'in' or 'at' work. The nature of their work, how they experience it, including those they work with and for, has a significant impact on the quality of their life, both inside and outside of work. A further focus of this book is to promote a better understanding of careers for people at any point in their career journey: entry, and exit or transition. This approach to careers is vital for everyone, including line and human resource managers, career counsellors and the like and not least students of career management.[2] However, a career experience is how a person feels, thinks and interprets it. People create, recreate or pioneer a career based on their understanding of it. The career experience is important as it provides self-direction and personal responsibility (Hall, 2002). As shown in Fig. 1 above, the experience of a career is influenced and mediated by many stakeholders who provide meaning and identity for the primary stakeholder.

THE CHANGING WORKFORCE

In most industrialised societies, people enter the workforce anywhere from their mid-teens onwards, and in many countries with the abolition of the statutory retirement age, now work beyond 65 years or longer, out of need or preference.[3] As in the past, it is the younger generations entering the workforce for the first time today who are the forerunners in a rapidly changing knowledge-driven, global economy.

Cultures influence thinking so the events that occur in the formative years from infancy to late adulthood of each generation shape actions, attitudes and norms. Some generations experience the same milestone events, albeit through a different lens depending on their life span (Gladding & Martin, 2010).

The younger generations will be most impacted as work and careers continue to be restructured driven by market and technological forces, even though much older generation remain career-focussed for much longer than their predecessors. The most pressing issues arising from this change include:

(a) workforce demographics and composition;

(b) flexibility and casualization;

(c) technological change: supplementing, replacing skills, people and workplaces;

(d) cultural change and diversity – workers from culturally diverse backgrounds, workplace, workforce and labour market;

(e) work anywhere, anytime with full access to systems;

(f) work practices focussed on outcomes and less on the process; and

(g) changing focus on work and life balance.

All of the above developments have implications for capacity and skill building requirements in careers. These requirements are important for addressing the fluidity of consumer demands; labour market planning in specific industries; government regulation and policies around workforce planning. Some industries are experiencing significant skill gaps; for example, just over 50 per cent of open positions are vacant due to the skills shortage in the US manufacturing industry (BLS Data, 2018). These trends are likely to continue unless the disparity between accessible talent and the skills required for the digital age are addressed. The growth of employment of younger people between the age of 15 and 29 years is slowing relative to other age cohorts. The distribution of the workforce also varies, with people preferring opportunities in metropolitan areas compared to rural, regional ones.

The bulk of the workforce now comprises Millennials and Gen X, with the numbers of baby boomers in decline. However, it is the millennial generation, people born between 1980 and 1994, which is the most significant proportion of the workforce (Weinbaum, Girven, & Oberholtzer, 2016).

In the workplace, people from diverse generations ultimately form bonds across the age boundaries, identifying with those younger or older through shared experiences, memories and symbols (Parry & Urwin, 2011). While a lot has been written about generational differences in the workforce, stereotypes propagated within the last several decades are generally fallacious (Pfau, 2016). Research shows that more similarities exist among the various generations than differences (Macky et al., 2008). A misconception that Baby Boomers and older generations do not have the appropriate technological and Internet-based skills is also refuted (Menyen & Adair, 2013).

Generational differences have more to do with career and life stage as well as the personal approach (Constanza, Badger, Fraser, Severt, & Gade, 2012). This perspective is essential in thinking about careers. After all, most people, regardless of their generation, are motivated similarly, although the ordering of priorities will vary depending on the career stage. Five motivations that are generic include the need for:

(1) productive work,

(2) compensation for work,

(3) secure employment,

(4) enriching tasks and

(5) skills and knowledge development.

Another difference to focus on is the acculturation and integration of new employees with the existing workforce in terms of the support that both may require, mainly if work is distributed and virtual.

WORK, WORKING AND WORKPLACES

Most generations around the world have witnessed extraordinary change such as the developments following WWI and the 1940s following WWII, moving from an agrarian social order to one of mass production (Polyani, 1944). This change was substantial, socially, technologically and politically. For the next few decades, careers were forged through bureaucratisation, functionalisation and specialisation, and as people took on these careers, life was routinised around work. Work became somewhat more predictable, and people's expectations aligned with this reality. Institutions employing large numbers of people, many with a career for life, were the foundation of the twentieth century, supported by governments, business and the community. People had a strong belief and their experience at work and the trajectory of their career became the map for future generations. The acceptance of this expectedness screened out the inherent, unpredictable nature of sociotechnical and political change. However, careers today are not extrapolations from the past or even the present.

The Internet of Things

Today, work, working and workplaces are characterised by the Internet of Things, mobile technologies, rapid-speed Internet access, all of which are impacting the nature and scheduling of work, its design and the use of work space. An increasing number of work-related activities are now automated, and this process will continue to escalate. Further, the use of artificial intelligence, for example, chatbots to serve online consumers, virtual and augmented reality as well as robotics are increasingly used to provide wide-ranging functions including human services, although the interface between people and robots remains at a relatively nascent stage.

The Internet continues to shape work significantly as well as workers and workplaces. Employers use the Internet for recruitment and selection, and a range of other human resource processes, including monitoring staff. It is not surprising that people need to consider the purpose and methods of employing the Internet to represent them professionally and career-wise. The Internet is central to developing an online presence. Opportunities abound through the Internet, which provides:

(a) a context for career building by canvassing, curating and using resources and information;

(b) learning about skills and labour markets, particularly online ones;

(c) an opportunity to promote an individual as well as; and

(d) connections.

Globalisation

Globalisation forged by competition is driving change. Globalisation augments the socio-cultural inter-connectedness, which is having ramifications for political and economic thinking and trends as well as financial, and market assimilations (Czinkota & Ronkainen, 2005). While globalisation processes provide new business and employment opportunities for organisations, they also contribute to destabilising conventional ways of organising work and people, such as:

(a) relocating industrial workplaces between nations and continents;

(b) replacing work carried out by people with robots and artificial intelligence technologies in production processes;

(c) new forms of the employer–employee relationship, for example, unpaid internships and other forms of work-integrated learning, casualisation and a rise in independent contracting; and

(d) people's certainty about the future has been disrupted; some are awake to this; many are not.

Access to Work

Currently, work functions as a considerable part of a person's life for physical, psychological and social well-being. What happens at work can affect all three aspects of a person's life.

Correspondingly, access to work is central to this and has a major impact when a person finds themselves unexpectedly out of work and also for the long-term unemployed. Society is at an energising stage concerning the future of work, with concerns that, if not carefully and thoughtfully managed, it will lead to increasing unemployment, underemployment, inequality and instability across many parts of the world.

In summary, careers are forged by ubiquitous change: environmentally, politically, socially and technologically, which sometimes invalidates power bases, customs and attitudes, often concealing the initial precipitating factors. These triggering factors include climatic conditions, government turnovers, wars, trade disputes, immigration, policies, regulations, as well as new technologies and digitisation.

THE SOCIOLOGY OF CAREERS

Work and careers shape the economy, the community and the society in which people live and raise families or not as they choose.

How work is arranged at the macro- and micro-levels in terms of the nature of work tasks performed by some and not others depending on their skill sets, what activities belong to specific industry sectors and organisations and not others, constitute not only employment relationships but also careers. Careers are a function of various factors, including political, socio-cultural, legal and economic policies and influence a person's internalisation of norms, rules and incentives.

When work and technology were more straightforward, it was assumed that specific tasks required specific skills, knowledge and experience. A simple view of work is disappearing, and with it, the role that career plays today in society. Contributing to this shift are the changing expectations about work, working, and people varying according to the generational lens of the observer, for example, Y, Z Alpha and those coming behind them.

As stated above up until now, careers were governed by the requirements specified by industry, industrial or professional associations not only stipulating standards of skills and knowledge of entrants but also providing an identity, an acknowledgment of skills or the rights to work in specific occupational domains. Changing career trends have significant implications for learning new knowledge and skills, which are shaped and delivered by key stakeholders mentioned earlier, such as employers, universities, colleges and schools. While some of these career features will remain, many will change as technology and hence knowledge widens, accelerates and diversifies.

Boundaryless Knowledge

Today, careers are tending towards boundaryless knowledge domains, meaning people require transdisciplinary knowledge, whether working individually or in groups or both. Currently, some careers are now tending more towards interdisciplinary and in the not-too-distant future, will be transdisciplinary, creating links among knowledge domains in a theoretical and practical sense (Brandt et al., 2013). This trend will significantly change how careers develop.

Disciplinary knowledge is continuing to disrupt as prevailing theories are overturned, revised, integrated and reconciled with newer thinking. To do so, after all, is the mission of academics and researchers working in these areas. The process of change at the theory level involves critical questioning, which is at the heart of the Socratic Method, reframing and applying assertive interrogation. At the same time, knowledge is politically constructed by governments in setting policies and in funding particular streams and types of research and development as well as organising relational power globally, nationally and locally with strategic stakeholders.

Careers assume knowledge, skills, remuneration, security, identity, meaning, position and so on. All of these components are valorised in particular ways and ingrained forming assumptions about what and how to learn, to work as well as notions of merit, equality and so on. Careers are also understood in terms of what they produce or contribute to society; the methods they use; and the processes of change such as professionalisation, specialisation and skill development. Questions to address this situation include the following:

(a) What, why and how are new ways of knowing and 'actionable' knowledge being produced?

(b) Who and what are those key stakeholders wish people to know? How can diverse views that inevitably arise, be reconciled?

(c) Are the current conventions of thinking about careers going to serve future generations well?

Roles are categorised as follows:

(i) Functional roles: performing and directed towards the goals that employers want to achieve.

(ii) Emotional roles: serving the goals or demands of the client, customer or student.

(iii) Ancillary roles: supporting either one of the above or both.

INNOVATION AND CAREERS

Since the late twentieth century, specialism has been a defining tenet of careers. While traditional, craft skills are relevant in specialist niché markets, they are not sustainable. For example, a hand crafted skill or product is converted to a mass scale production if there is a demand. A foremost difference today compared to the past is that consumers and the community generally value environmentally justifiable products and services as well as democratic rights at work, including the freedom of speech. Social responsibility has become the defining tenet of the twenty-first century to date and is discussed in Chapter 6.

Apart from the individual skill contribution, employers aim to exploit technological innovation, demand or value chains and most importantly, intellectual capital and property rights. Brand value is increasingly important for employers for the organisations they represent and also for people in terms of their brand and reputation.

Knowledge and skills transfer in the workplace is vital (Zhu, Chiu, & Infante Holguin-Veras, 2018). While the value of learning has heightened among career stakeholders, a university degree is more likely to be seen as less valuable than specific and relevant skills or experience. Most employers aim to develop an agile learning environment for staff (Annosi, Hemphälä, & Brunetta, 2018). Employees are expected to contribute to the learning in organisations hence the notion of agility through knowledge sharing. A rising number of organisations are developing agile learning (Gan, Menkhoff, & Smith, 2015) and developing knowledge management channels to provide effective systems and practices for the sharing and use of the knowledge by employees (Brantingham, Brantingham, & Kinney, 2017). People are potentially as agile as the organisations in which they work, and this is acknowledged (Noguera, Guerrero-Roldán, & Masó, 2018).

Work is designed around projects and once completed, people move to the next destination. In addition to creativity and innovation skills, the ability to negotiate and command financial incentives as well as knowing employee rights will be the drivers of careers and career transitions. As the linear career come to an end, insights into the value of specific skills and ways of working over others will translate into 'portfolio careers'.

For employers who wish to retain people, work integrated learning is core. There is another reason related to the degree of uncertainty that people, employers and consumers are facing: adaptability, which will require continuous education, retraining and skill rotation. Job mobility will be part of the agile approach, and therefore, employers have a pertinent role to play in this, so that society is not confronting industry closures, large-scale redundancies and the like without people being prepared to transition and access new opportunities. In many ways, it is revisiting the past debates around skill which have never been realised fully in practice. Increasingly, people want not only to contribute and have greater autonomy at work but also to make a difference. To contribute to the greater good is aspirational for most people.

CAREER ATTRIBUTES

Undoubtedly, careers are becoming more flexible, which benefit consumers, employers and workers in different ways. Place, distance, and time are reflected in the way work is designed, more or less flexibly, as shown in Table 1.

Table 1 reflects some key design criteria employed to structure workers, work and, by default, careers. For example, employers control over where people work, how work is organised, that is, the division of labour and the allocation of tasks and projects, work functions and groups, ownership of

Table 1. Work Design Criteria.

Who	Why	Place and Distance	Time	Focus	How	Measures
Business owner	Purpose	Workplace	Virtual	Services	Theory	Productivity
Employer	Passion	Office	Actual	Product	Applied	Knowledge
Manager	Balanced with	Hot desk		Project	Routine	Skill
Worker Employee	other demands	Vehicle		Task	Non-routine	Effort
Contractor		Home		Processes		Compliance
Casual		Remote work hub				
				Customer		
				Client		
				Patient		
				Student		
				Community		
			Full-time		Solo	
			Part-time		Joint	
			As required		Collaborative	

the work space such as work stations or enclosed offices. These parameters shape work and career cultures; for example, if work is open space, communication among workers may increase with greater opportunities for a collaborative culture.

Second, distance is viewed in terms of proximity to the principal 'place' of work, closeness to other workers, that is, relationships required to get the work done, such as serving customers in a 'bricks and mortar' location or online, as well as the nature of control between supervisor and subordinate as well as their work output.

Third, time is viewed in terms of the passage of work between workers and functions; standardising work tasks as well as the amount of time spent in working, linked both to a worker's productivity and commitment.

Fourth, redesigning work is aimed at the sustainability of productivity and service delivery, including its responsiveness to changing the market and workplace demands. It has implications for how work is organised, work roles constructed and delineated task design and delegation, and individual versus group work or indeed, automated processes, hence task replacement.

The form of employment in Australia is more varied now, with an increase in the diversity of employment types other than the 'traditional' arrangement of a full-time, ongoing wage or salary job, with regular hours and paid leave (Australian Bureau of Statistics, 2012). The design of work is essentially a cultural artefact of the work organisation primarily, devised by managerial rules based on assumptions of place, distance and time. However, it has far-reaching implications for people and careers and its impact on structuring future options for people to engage in and benefit from work. What happens in the work organisation has implications for industries. For example, introducing flexible and remote working (FRW) into the work organisation is often a cost-saving benefit for the organisation. Digital workplaces are also transforming work and workers.

This intervention is likely to have an impact on their engagement, performance and retention at work. Performance is usually digitally monitored reminiscent of 'Bundy clocks' used in many organisations to measure people's time at work.

Increasingly careers, like work, are less likely tied to a physical location or traditional hours, with some exceptions in the human services industries including retail. However, many of these functions are being replaced by online shopping and will be increasingly automated in place too. People now work different shifts or travel schedules; share desks or office space; replacing private offices with open spaces with team rooms or work stations. 'Hoteling' is the new buzz word for serviced and fully-equipped office space provided by the lease. Office spaces are booked and open to anyone regardless of position in the organisation. A 'concierge' may provide travel and logistical support. Satellite offices are another form of the workplace, located where people are more likely to reside. Given the ageing population, more people want inhome services to meet their needs and not only health care. Working from home is the most common form of substitute workplaces, especially when people have rapid Internet access to enable all the things they need to do, including collaborating with persons and colleagues.

While in the past, physical workplaces have been important mutually for professional and social reasons, both impacting a person's career. Place, distance and time, therefore:

(a) are situated deep within organisational and work practices, making them less readily observable;

(b) reside within existing power bases (e.g. management and unions) in the workplace; and

(c) are linked to people' desire, located in the managerial hierarchy, to protect their interests and job security.

Work is a socialising activity and intrinsically rewarding for most people. However, today, people face a paradox where workplaces are downsizing and virtual work is becoming increasingly common place, there is less opportunity for people to meet in person. Rather than deemphasising the need for collaboration, it is now an imperative, although it may take a different form and pattern to the past. Coupled with this are the changing skill dynamics and the fact that knowledge is both explicit and tacit.

Building a sense of workplace community has its benefits. If well organised, it is intrinsically gratifying, providing staff with a sense of security and well-being. An individual's sense of community is primarily through work today and may only be through an online community in some cases, of membership and belonging in a friendship network at work, becomes part of one's self-concept and augments the individual's sense of purpose in life. Finally, as a base element of social support, it may enhance a worker's coping ability and buffer work demands. A sense of community has been shown to improve the health of employees by reducing stress and increasing social support.

The more connected people are digitally, some may feel more disconnected and separate from the action. To attest to this, generally speaking, communities are seeing a decline in civic engagement, for example (Volunteer Snapshot, 2015), engagement in clubs, religious organisations and other social institutions. Connectedness at work has become more valuable and particularly the ability to work and communicate in teams.

Where working is remote for some people and given that people are mostly relationally motivated, they will need to work harder at connecting so that they get a sense of who they are as well as their capabilities. It is an art in itself to be part of a working culture with negligible physically contact.

Work design shapes the workplace culture, which is changing as are people's interests and power bases. People go to work for contact with others as much as for the doing of the work. Work and careers are relational. Working with others, building relationships, gaining trust and understanding is important, especially as more and more people will work virtually, anytime and anywhere. However, providing people with choice around their work flexibility is vital for career progression and development.

Dimensions of place, distance and time provide valuable insights into careers and career choices.

IS THE NOTION OF CAREER ON ITS WAY OUT?

As society restructures and its labour markets become more diverse, the notion of a career is changing too. Values, attitudes, institutions, infrastructure as well as actions and practices have also changed overtime and will continue to do so. People are wary about these changes as some lament the loss of career stability and security of the past. People, when confronted with change, often become fixated on the negative aspects understandably rather than taking control and thinking about future opportunities and, in particular, career directions, noting that this is likely to be multidirectional. However, it is premature to declare that a career is merely a relic of the past.

Career thinking is a viable process (skill or tool) for managing career change. It requires the harnessing of creative thinking and innovation and replacing the idea that there is one career for each person. People need to think in multiple careers, many of which will require transdisciplinary skills and perspectives.

SOLUTIONISM – A QUICK FIX

While 'solutionism' proposes a technology fix for most problems (Morozov, 2014), what will this mean for careers? With the rapid development of technology and globalisation, it is apposite to ask under what guise career development will take in the future. As the career context has shifted over time, the understanding of career development has changed. This trend, which is likely to gather momentum in the future, raises some thought-provoking questions. In the face of significant change, it is paradoxical and yet understandable that governments, in general, have become more risk averse in creative policy development for workforce planning. While no one has a crystal ball to see future careers, a strategy needs to be in place to manage multiple transitions.

Solutionism manifests itself in the way that if people perceive 'disruptive innovation', they normalise it, seeing it as inevitable and innately positive. They respond by trying to determine a technological fix and this weighs heavily on people's capacity to investigate and tackle complex problems. In many ways, today's generations have moved along way from the Socratic Method (based on Morozov, 2014). The 'will to improve' (Li, 2007) assumes that change is needed to enhance productivity and profits and that all consequences of a technological change will benefit everyone. Second, the 'digital revolution' is the answer to society's problems and devolving to an Uber-driven society (de Saille & Medvecky, 2016).

While many theoretical underpinnings of work, organisations and careers have moved to accommodate these changes, the thinking that underpins careers essentially remains unmoved. There is a need to re-think career development in terms of who 'owns' it? Is this solely the domain of educational institutions? If so, are they obligated to collaborate more closely on what this means for future pathways into employment and careers? Or, is it in the domain of employers who in recent times has disowned 'career pathways' leaving it to individuals to progress their careers? This book sees career development as a strategy, and like most strategies, it requires a collaborative input as all stakeholders benefit if people work in satisfying careers.

Finding solutions to career conundrums are both essential and instructive. Popper's (2002) idea of finding solutions was through two fundamental principles: inference and disproof (i.e. a falsification process). He believed that people are engaged in problem solving as a way of existing (Hansen, 2007). In work, finding new ways of doing things is a central motivation. Applying a Popperian perspective (2002), inventions, whether substantive or ethereal, are initiated by the identification of such, followed by critique and validation. In the course of creativity, new problems emerge requiring an attempt to resolve inevitable conflicting ideas, an essential part of creative thinking as well as investigating and recognising unsettling questions (Hansen, 2007). Designing new forms of work and technology come to light through this fundamental process involving science and imagination. Careers need to be forged similarly and career prototyping is the topic of Chapter 5.

However, there is an apparent contradiction in solutionism, pertinent for careers and notions of work autonomy versus collectivity. Philosophers such as Kant (Nenon, 2014), Locke (Priselac, 2016) and Hobbes (Courtland, 2017) compared agency and dignity with the person's rational self-awareness and their capacity to act independently from others (Prainsack, 2017). In terms of careers, people work and forge careers within a network of relations. What people need are new ways of working and new methods for dealing with uncertainty and ambiguity. Business as usual thinking, especially about careers is no longer sustainable. Freire (2000) referred to the importance of construction and reconstruction as 'problem posing'.

EDUCATION – THE PROBLEM OR SOLUTION?

The 'cultural logic of late capitalism' (Jameson, 1991) suggests that solutions are found either through education or some other means. Education has long been used to frame social problems as learning ones and performs an imperative function in addressing social issues and providing opportunities. Similarly, education has been hailed as the 'solution' to the career conundrum.

> ... *the promise of new and ever-more sophisticated technics not only drives capitalist consumerism in the West but is readily evoked as the pretence that new and as-yet-unimagined technologies will miraculously emerge at some future date to remedy problems that are perceived as too difficult and too expensive to remedy in the present. (MacLellan, 2013, p. 160)*

Individuals, at perhaps the most formative time of their lives, not only are burdened with paying for their education but also the responsibility of finding a career in a world which is changing rapidly and over which they feel to have little control. Learning is more effective when it reflects real-world practice experiences of participants as well as open interaction between educators, employers and the participants themselves.

Today, in developed countries, most young people attend school, with an increasing percentage engaging in further or higher education and eventually transition to work. However, as mentioned earlier, unemployment for people aged, 16–24 years, in high-income countries, including the EU, the US, the UK and Australia is rising to three times that of adult rates (International Labour Office, 2014). For young people, the cost to their mental, physical and financial health is high.

In an average generation, the direct cost to the UK public sector is about £56,500–104,300 (IMPETUS, 2017). The rise in youth unemployment and the probability of job displacement impacting employment for all adults is a significant concern for future careers. It is apparent that more needs to be done to forge an inextricable link between education, business and the labour market.

Education is viewed as a 'fix' that is instrumental in developing skills in graduates so that they are productive. This view is short-sighted as, given the changing nature of work and careers, the shelf-life of skills is short-lived. Fig. 2 shows the capability continuum in a period of career disruption and how it impacts all levels of capability.

Culturally responsive curriculum and pedagogy are instrumental, especially in this era of disrupted careers. People need to be able to imagine 'success-likely' futures and develop capabilities to allow them to function effectively

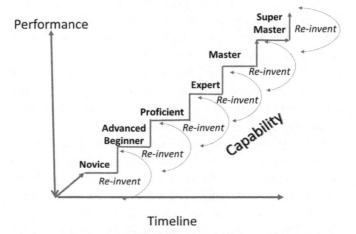

Fig. 2.   Capability Continuum in a Period of Career Disruption.

within them. Instead of using the starting point of getting a job or a narrowly defined view of talent and relationships, people need to be able to imagine and design their future careers. If so, a knowledgeable and specialised capability is understood and valued as a social benefit rather than a purely individual one.

Education is crucial for developing people's capacity to tackle complex challenges, although not in terms of more of the same. Further, an instrumental view of education over-looks the value of learning to assist people in questioning their assumptions, beliefs and value systems and how these align with those with society (Simons & Masschelein, 2005). When people engage in deep learning that is structured scaf-fold learning over a sustained period, they are more prepared in terms of critical and hence, open to considering change (Tawfik et al., 2018).

There are various ways to think about the value of learning, including:

(a) a sociological standpoint: social benefits;

(b) an economic outlook: supply and demand;

(c) a linguistic perspective: nuanced meanings; and

(d) a personal view (Graeber, 2001).

Value is recognised as 'the way people who could do almost anything (including, in the right circumstances, create entirely new sorts of social relations) and assess the importance of what they do' (Graeber, 2001, p. 47). For example, most uni-versities and colleges have established innovation and entre-preneurship programmes to assist students to enhance their inventiveness, using and building their knowledge, skills and attitudes. The invention facilitates applying imagination to real-world thinking to their own lives and is highly motivating

(Silverblatt, Ferry, & Finan, 1999). This is a pertinent course for individuals imagining their future careers and has implications for support from the government, education, business and the community.

Is it time to further emphasise and reappraise education and shift the focus from a purely individual perspective to one where people collaborate more to consider issues from a transdisciplinary perspective and globally in an economic, social, technical, educational and political sense? Collaboration, connecting with others and being courageous to release educational futures frees career thinking from the constraints of socio-deterministic and competitive thinking.

Developing people's capabilities from critical thinking to social cooperation will not only contribute, social and economic benefits, but also provide meaningful and productive work as well as a personal acknowledgement. These factors have always been important and will take on renewed emphasis in the decades ahead. Chapters four and five provide further amplification of this issue.

THE WAY FORWARD

Career development is a foremost challenge for individuals, educators, employers and society as a whole. One of the things that makes it thorny is that careers are experienced in various ways by different generations, industries, occupations and so on. Notwithstanding this, there are some standard dimensions: demands of skill, knowledge, workload, control, support, relationships, role, change and work-life balance. Most careers contain elements of the task, transactional and relationship focussed activities as well as undergoing some form of transition and transformation.

While there is no halting change, it requires new thinking and learning, refreshing a portfolio of skills to help guide people to survey future career horizons, canvass options, narratives of transformative action, developing a risk appetite. Risk is the 'probability distribution of the consequences of each alternative' March and Simon (1958), whereas uncertainty is 'the consequences of each alternative belong to some subset of all possible consequences, but that the decision maker cannot assign definite probabilities to the occurrence of particular outcomes' (Alessandri, Ford, Lander, Leggio, & Taylor, 2004). Understanding that career will be an as much a collective phenomenon as it has been institutional and individual in the past is important.

While people's understanding of careers once depended on understanding the past, this is no longer entirely true. Thinking about the future of careers does not rely on reconstructing history. Enough has been done on that already, suffice to say that in the past the focus of career centred upon industry, hierarchy, development and men. The task ahead is not a futile one as is often projected. Society itself is evolving and has been transforming from a world governed by career elites into a society where all voices will vie for attention. Societal transformation requires boomeranging to the future rather than being anchored in the present.

Change alters people's perceptions and opinions about how they work and the career choices they make (Jhagroe & Frantzeskaki, 2016), apart from the noticeable effects and effects of change. This requires interpreting change by putting things into perspective, a critical skill, especially for those seeking to start or sustain a career. The ability to think analytically about change, including having a healthy risk appetite and tolerance for ambiguity is critical for building self-confidence to deal with establishing a career, career change as well as making suitable career choices.

UNCERTAINTY OR CERTAINTY: OPPORTUNITY OR CONSTRAINT?

Career development is now essential and not incidental if talent sustainability is going to be harnessed. The recognition that a genuine effort supporting career development is central to the talent and the employer value proposition. Communities of practice shape skill development that individuals can tap into. Social media, matrixed arrangements and project-based work have produced talent and mentoring pools that people can draw from. These processes are also ideal for people building their career pathways.

This complexity and a heightened perception of uncertainty co-exist with the belief that people participate in knowledge societies. Knowledge is a conceptual canopy that delineates how work and social life is organised and resources used. Embedded practices are derived from experience and are motivated by interests, values, beliefs and assumptions. What is knowledge, and what is it to know something?

Being change-wise is vital for addressing the challenges that lie ahead. Work and career feature prominently in everyone's lives, whether in paid or unpaid employment. It commences from the time people first consider 'what will I be when I grow up?'

The future of careers is a theme of considerable debate within all industries in first world countries today. Notwithstanding this, there is much to learn about how careers will play out in the future for individuals and society as a whole. Given the dramatic rise in technological, economic and market changes and disruption in all spheres, including the political, the outcome is unpredictable.

This situation demands new streams of thinking to contest existing models left over from the twentieth century towards innovating strategies to address the new socio-economic and political demands of the careers of the future. Career development is aimed at how people manage this information as well as the impressions that they form to bring about the opportunities to create entirely new careers.

The demand for expertise and career development has never been more critical than it is right now. The hastening of change in the workplace transformation requires continuous skill development and re-invention too. Employers and governments have much to do to advance skills and deliver career development to current and future generations. This demand is often overlooked, particularly by employers in favour of things that are revenue intensive, a theme of the final chapter.

OUTLINE OF THIS BOOK

Chapter 2 explores self-transformation through career development and narratives to assist in making sense of what is going on in a person's world. Social evolution and changing careers are both socially constructed and in turn, influence career makers those creating the change, leading to different kinds of roles and different kinds of presences for career incumbents. The upshot is that as careers progress into the future, they may offer people more options than previously available or considered. It covers how careers transform along three dimensions – intrapersonal, social and cognitive – that together create a unified concept.

Chapter 3 focusses on career strategising to inform career choice, design and outcomes. However, in careers, as anyone knows who has engaged in career planning, this relationship is problematic. It is taking a 'wide angle' view of the world of opportunities. More significantly, it is the ability to act creatively, that is, to be open to possibilities and acquire a healthy risk appetite under these circumstances is also prudent.

Chapter 4 outlines design thinking, a way of creating new career options. It is also a process that people in many industries use to design solutions, products, services, etc. Here it is used to address the needs of stakeholders who benefit from careers. As such, through the generation of new ideas, people gain new insights and balance diverse perspectives into a whole, that is, integrative thinking.

Chapter 5 considers and develops a way to elicit opportunities to organise career that create value for career incumbents and their associated stakeholders. Realising how to articulate what the incumbent knows in terms of designing a career to assist them in realising their career purpose. For prototyping, there are different emphases, including identifying and refining career identity, career relationships as well as information needs and resources.

Chapter 6 turns attention away from career decision making processes to focus on the role of employers in establishing organisational practices for the sustainability of careers. The chapter includes a discussion about how in times of change, the development of advanced technologies and digitisation, and an uncertain future, is causing concern. Questions are posed such as how society can ensure that technological development often leading to disruption occurs without dampening the potential and most importantly, the career aspirations and realities of current and future generations.

Corporate social responsibility (CSR) is critical to business strategy. Employers are important influences of CSR practices. On this issue, boards and executive management need to ensure that they act in the best interests of the wider community in which they reside to guarantee environmental, social, cultural, legal and ethical safeguards (Aguinis & Glavas, 2012). Currently, career equity seems to be one issue that both metropolitan and regional communities value. Employment, unemployment and careers are foremost in people's minds, especially when voting a government in or out.

NOTES

1. Based on Robert Frost poem 'The Road not Taken' 1916

2. Career counsellors need to ensure they have wide and deep work experience as well as industry connections to provide real value.

3. In developing countries, the working age is much younger.

REFERENCES

Aguinis, H., & Glavas, A. (2012). What we know and don't know about corporate social responsibility: A review and research agenda. *Journal of Management, 38*(4), 932–968.

Alessandri, T., Ford, D., Lander, D., Leggio, K., & Taylor, M. (2004). Managing risk and uncertainty in complex capital projects. *The Quarterly Review of Economics and Finance, 44*, 751–767.

Annosi, M. C., Hemphälä, J., & Brunetta, F. (2018). Investigating the impact of agile methods on learning and innovation. In P. Boccardelli, M. Annosi, F. Brunetta, & M. Magnusson (Eds.), *Learning and innovation in hybrid organisations* (pp. 73–97). Cham, Switzerland: Palgrave Macmillan.

Arnold, J., & Jackson, C. (1997). The new career: Issues and challenges. *British Journal of Guidance & Counselling, 25*(4), 427–433.

Australian Bureau of Statistics. (2012). *Year book Australia 2012*. Canberra, Australia: ABS.

BLS Data. (2018). Deloitte skills gap and future of work in the manufacturing study. Retrieved from https://www2.deloitte.com

Brandt, P., Ernst, A., & Gralla, F., & Luederitz, C. (2013). A review of transdisciplinary research in sustainability science. *Ecological Economics*, *92*, 1–15.

Brantingham, P., Brantingham, P., & Kinney, B. (2017). Criminology in Canada: The context of its criminology. In R. A. Triplett (Ed.), *The handbook of the history and philosophy of criminology* (pp. 360–376). Hoboken, NJ: John Wiley & Sons.

Cohen, L. E. (2013). Assembling jobs: A model of how tasks are bundled in and across jobs. *Organisation Science*, *24*, 432–454.

Constanza, D. P., Badger, J. M., Fraser, R. L., Severt, J. B., & Gade, P. A. (2012). Generational differences in work-related attitudes: A meta-analysis. *Journal of Business and Psychology*, *27*, 375–394.

Courtland, S. D. (2017). *Hobbesian applied ethics and public policy*. London: Routledge.

Czinkota, M. R., & Ronkainen, I. A. (2005). A forecast of globalisation, international business and trade: Report from a Delphi study. *Journal of World Business*, *40*(2), 111–123.

de Saille, S., & Medvecky, F. (2016). Innovation for a steady state: a case for responsible stagnation. *Economy and Society*, *45*(1), 1–23.

Freire, P. (2000). In M. B. Ramos (Trans.), *Pedagogy of the oppressed*. New York, NY: Continuum.

Frost, R., Untermeyer, L., & Frost, R. (1991). *The road not taken: A selection of Robert Frost's poems*. New York, NY: H. Holt and Co.

Gan, B., Menkhoff, T., & Smith, R. (2015). Enhancing students' learning process through interactive digital media:

New opportunities for collaborative learning. *Computers in Human Behaviour*, *51*, 652–663.

Gell, A. (1992). In J. Coote, & A. Shelton (Eds.), *The technology of enchantment and the enchantment of technology, in anthropology, art, and aesthetics* (pp. 40–63). Oxford: Oxford University Press.

Gladding, S. T., & Martin, B. (2010). Creativity and self-esteem in later life. In M. H. Guindon (Ed.), *Self-esteem across the lifespan* (pp. 311–323). New York, NY: Routledge.

Graeber, D. (2001). *Toward an anthropological theory of value* (pp. 1–2). New York, NY: Palgrave.

Greenhaus, J., Callanan, G. A., & Godschalk, V. M. (2010). *Career management*. Thousand Oaks, CA: Sage.

Gubler, M., Arnold, J., & Coombs, C. (2014). Organisational boundaries and beyond: A new look at the components of a boundaryless career orientation. *Career Development International*, *19*, 641–667.

Hall, D. T. (2002). *Careers in and out of organisations*. Thousand Oaks, CA: Sage Publication.

Hansen, T. E. (ed.). (2007). In A. Pickel (trans.), *The two fundamental problems of the theory of knowledge*. London: Routledge.

Jameson, F. (1991). *Postmodernism, or, the cultural logic of late capitalism*. Durham, NC: Duke University Press.

Jhagroe, S., & Frantzeskaki, N. (2016). Framing a crisis: Exceptional democracy in Dutch infrastructure governance. *Critical Policy Studies*, *10*(3), 348–364.

IMPETUS. (2017). *Private equity foundation. Youths job index. August 2017*. United Kingdom: IMPETUS Private Equity Foundation.

International Labour Office. (2014). *Global employment trends 2014: Risk of a jobless recovery?* Geneva, Switzerland: ILO.

Khapova, S. N., & Arthur, M. B. (2011). Interdisciplinary approaches to contemporary career studies. *Human Relations, 64*(1), 3–17.

Li, T. (2007). *The will to improve: Governmentality, development, and the practice of politics.* Duke: Duke University Press.

Macky, K., Gardner, D., & Forsyth, S. (2008). Generational differences at work: Introduction and overview. *Journal of Managerial Psychology, 23*(8), 857–861.

MacLellan, M. (2013). Capitalism's many futures: A brief history of theorising post-capitalism technologically. *Mediations, 26,* 159–160.

March, J. G., & Simon, H. A. (1958). *Organisations.* New York, NY: Wiley.

McDonald, K. S., & Hite, L. M. (2008). The next generation of career success. Implications for HRD. *Advances in Developing Human Resources, 10*(1), 86–103.

McMahon, M., Watson, M., & Lee, M. (2019). Qualitative career assessment: A review and reconsideration. *Journal of Vocational Behaviour, 110,* 420–432.

Menyen, T., & Adair, T. (2013). Understanding senior Australians and their communities: Findings from a nationwide survey. Melbourne, Australia: National Seniors Productive Ageing Centre.

Moore, C., Gunz, H., & Hall, D. T. (2007). Tracing the roots of career theory in management and organisational studies.

In H. Gunz & M. Peiperl (Eds.), *Handbook of career studies Los Angeles*. CA: Sage Publications.

Morozov, E. (2014). *To save everything, click here: The folly of technological, solutionism*. New York, NY: Public Affairs.

Nenon, T. (2014). *Kant, Kantianism, and idealism: The origins of continental philosophy* (1st ed.). London: Routledge.

Noguera, I., Guerrero-Roldán, A.-E., & Masó, R. (2018). Collaborative agile learning in online environments: Strategies for improving team regulation and project management. *Computers & Education, 116*, 110–129.

Padgett, J. F. (2012). *The emergence of organisations and markets* (pp. 1–5). Princeton, NJ: Princeton University Press.

Parry, E., & Urwin, P. (2011). Generational differences in work values: A review of theory and evidence. *International Journal of Management Reviews, 13*, 79–96.

Patton, W., & McIlveen, P. (2009). Practice and research in career counselling and development – 2008. *Career Development Quarterly, 58*, 118–161.

Pfau, B. (2016). What do millennials really want at work? The same things as the rest of us. *Harvard Business Review*. Retrieved from https://hbr.org/2016/04/what-do-millennials-really-wantat-work.

Polyani, K. (1944). *The great transformation*. Boston: Second Beacon Paperback.

Polanyi, M. (1967). *The tacit dimension*. New York, NY: Anchor Books.

Popper, P. (2002). *The logic of scientific discovery* (2nd ed.). London: Routledge.

Prainsack, B. (2017). The "people" in the "me": Solidarity and health care in the era of personalised medicine. *Science, Technology, and Human Values*, *43*(1), 21–44.

Priselac, M. (2016). *Locke's science of knowledge*. London: Routledge.

Rousseau, D. M. (1995). *Psychological contracts in organizations: Understanding written and unwritten agreements*. Thousand Oaks, CA: Sage Publications.

Silverblatt, A., Ferry, J., & Finan, B. (1999). *Approaches to media literacy: A handbook*. London: M.E. Sharpe.

Simons, M., & Masschelein, J. (2005). In S. Tremain (Ed.), *An inclusive education for exclusive pupils: A critical analysis of the government of the exceptional* (pp. 208–228). Ann Arbor, MI: University of Michigan Press.

Tawfik, A. A., Law, V., Xun, G., Wanli, X. & Kim, K. (2018). The effect of sustained vs. faded scaffolding on students' argumentation in ill-structured problem solving. *Computers in Human Behaviour*, *1*, 1–14.

Turner, J. R. (2014). *The handbook of project-based management* (4th ed.). New York, NY: McGraw-Hill.

Volunteering Snapshot. (2015). Australian Bureau of Statistics. From the fourth General Social Survey. Retrieved from https://www.abs.gov.au/ausstats/abs@.nsf/mf/4159.0

Vondracek, F. W., Ford, D. H., & Porfeli, E. J. (2014). *A living systems theory of vocational behaviour and development*. Rotterdam: Sense Publishers.

Weinbaum, C., Girven, R., & Oberholtzer, J. (2016). *The millennial generation: Implications for the intelligence and policy communities*. Santa Monica, CA: Rand Corporation. Retrieved from https://www.rand.org/content/dam/rand/pubs/research_reports/RR1300/RR1306/RAND_RR1306.pdf

Zhu, Y. Q., Chiu, H., & Infante Holguin-Veras, E. J. (2018). It is more blessed to give than to receive: Examining the impact of knowledge sharing on sharers and recipients. *Journal of Knowledge Management, 22*(1), 76–91.

2

CAREER THINKING
COMPETENCE

INTRODUCTION

Thinking careers entails openness, self-awareness, critical reflection and support from others. Becoming competent in career thinking requires possessing knowledge about work, working, organisations and pathways. Competence requires the capacity to apply past learning, how and where to address problems in new situations (Glaser, 2001).

Competence in thinking encourages learning about beliefs, interests and practices that are different from one's own. However, an overblown belief in personal competence could segue into over-generalising and may be a barrier for being open to new ideas, self-awareness, critical reflection, accepting support or acknowledging individual preferences.

Consequently, career knowledge is insufficient for appreciating diverse working experiences, being receptive to consistent self-improvement and maturity. If this is the case, people may avoid investing in supportive relationships with others or redressing power imbalances due to structural biases.

In other words, a sense of competence could lead to incompetence, thwarting a questioning approach required for advancing career thinking and opportunities.

Careers are problematic – what Dewey also calls indeterminate – because it disrupts the balance or equilibrium born from successful habit (Dewey, 1941). 'There is a troubled, perplexed, trying situation, where the difficulty is, as it were, spread throughout the entire situation…' (Dewey 1933, p. 201). Often, what is assumed to be 'correct' or 'relevant' is not. Therefore, routine thinking needs to be disrupted to trigger an inquiry, action-orientated learning and ways to boost career development. If people engage principally in routine thinking, it blocks the need for an inquiry and camouflages knowledge or skill gaps falsely leading people to feel competent when their competence is being eroded.

Turning Point

Living a career often presents people with challenging and pivotal moments or situations, a turning point. 'Living a career' is a concept that leads to life-trajectories such as personal, occupational and biological milestones, for example, graduation, first job, committing to a life partner, starting a family, promotion and so on. All these milestones are time-based and do not necessarily progress as desired or planned and all the attendant consequences of this (based on Giele & Elder, 1998).

Turning points generate transformation. What prompts a turning point? An external event may lead to sparking an interest or an internal, emotional or cognitive, conflict for a person which may alter their values, beliefs, attitudes and actions (Druckman, Olekalns, & Smith, 2009). In determining one path over another, people begin to focus and re-frame some issues so that these are aligned to their purpose (Druckman and Olekalns, 2013). Both prompts are interlinked (Adair & Loewenstein, 2013).

The turning point is likely to expose a predicament or present a demand that when addressed adequately, allows the incumbent to understand what is going on and proffer something in return. The event demands attention, a response and often is the trigger point for change. How people address the incident is an essential trigger for learning about oneself and others and reveals their interests and agendas. For example, if a predicament at work is experienced by an individual as upsetting, it will instigate a sequence of events that lead to enhanced learning. A career journey is a means, or a chance, for personal change, psychological growth and transformation.

Transformation understands the 'self' not as a being in itself, rather as developing from social interactions and past experiences (based on Hermans, 2013). The self undergoes both internal and external changes. It involves allowing people to generate their motivation to drive them into the discovery and decision phase of their career lives.

Turning points and career transformations are best realised when incumbents confront challenging decisions when options are conflicted by external and internal factors or both. At these points, irrespective of where they are in their career journey or what path they have chosen, people realise the need to evaluate and weigh up the pros and cons of their options. They need to consider the impact of one option over another in terms of what it means for them personally and professionally. They are likely to consult with others, for example, a mentor or career coach, or a trusted significant other. When making choices, it matters to the decision-maker how others will regard the outcome both for the decision-maker as well as themselves, hence the link to both personal and professional identity. However, considering others' reactions often over-complicates the process and, overtime, people learn to navigate or negotiate their way through this complexity.

At work, people often confront quantitative requirements (e.g. workload) and qualitative ones (e.g. work complexity or ambiguity; satisfying the requirements of supervisor) while at the same time, coping with the needs of their personal lives (e.g. partner, children and elderly parents). Another factor in career decision making is considering an opportunity for career progression, like a promotion, and weighing up the demands of a new role in addition to existing demands, such as those outlined above.

Sometimes, people find themselves having to comply with the values and interests of their employer, which contradicts their own, creating an ethical quandary for them. This contradiction is more apparent for someone early rather than later in their career when they have to decide according to approved company policy, which seems blatantly unjust when applied to the person.

These contradictions trigger self-reflection, potential identity crisis and hence a search for making sense of what is the 'right thing to do'.

CAREER MINDFULNESS

Mindfulness allows people to explore their inner dimensions, including their mindsets, worldviews, beliefs, values and emotions, all of which contribute to a person's competence.

The qualities needed for career competence include being open to new ideas, self-awareness, engaging in supportive interactions, self-reflection and critique (based on Foronda, Baptiste, Reinholdt, & Ousman, 2016). These qualities originate from the experience of working long-term, in diverse contexts or both. Being open and receptive to new ideas and reconsidering fixed assumptions. Self-awareness requires introspection of one's dispositions, attitudes and practices. It involves mindfulness of one's own 'strengths, limitations, values, beliefs, actions and appearance to others' (Foronda et al., 2016, p. 211). The above qualities are important for engaging with others in a reciprocally positive way as well a way to ameliorate flaws and recognising the need to address gaps for self-improvement. There are direct links among a person's values, intentions and engagement as well as mindfulness and innovation (Ericson et al., 2014).

Reflective Thinking

Reflective thinking is the 'active desire' to consider multiple perspectives, especially those that are different from one's thoughts (Dewey, 1933, p. 136). Considering perspectives that are opposite to one's own or canvassing arguments for more than one possible decision outcome is a powerful learning and shapes the choices people make. Reflection is not an inconsequential practice with the aim to undergo change, especially at a career turning point (Dewey, 1933, p. 137). Regarding reflection, responsibility is accepting the actual consequences of one's actions, irrespective of good intentions, while similarly working towards remedies if the results of those actions are challenging.

There are several stages of reflection for addressing challenges, including:

(1) trigger thinking,

(2) proposing questions aimed at seeking resolution,

(3) developing a hypothesis to open and monitor observation especially of evidence,

(4) augmenting the issue based on 1–3 above and

(5) appraising it using imagination (based on Dewey, 1933, p.).

Failing to question one's thinking or 'old' knowledge can lead to single-loop learning (discussed in Chapter 4), leading to shallow remediation and, hence, a false sense of competence.

The scope of this chapter is to provide insight into the range of skills and tools for developing competence in career thinking. The goals of career thinking-competence imply the possibility of mastery, which conversely undermines the potential for gaining insight into a person's shortcomings and opportunity for growth. The practice of reflective thinking is discussed further below in this chapter and again in Chapter 3.

CULTURAL AND EMOTIONAL INTELLIGENCE

Cultural and emotional intelligence (EI) are interrelated and imperative for becoming 'career-wise' or intelligent. Cultural intelligence is 'a person's capability to adapt effectively to a new cultural context' (Earley, 2003, p. 274) and is established in understanding culture by being exposed to explicit cultural (intercultural) contexts. It is reliant on a person's self-awareness of the way they think about cultural diversity. Second, it includes how skilful a person is in responding effectively to other people in culturally diverse situations different to one's own. Cultural intelligence converges on a collection of abilities and not desired behaviours (Ang et al., 2007).

Emotions and EI are vital for actualising capabilities towards searching, attaining and sustaining careers.

> *Emotional intelligence is a kind of social*
> *intelligence that enables individuals to monitor the*
> *motions of others and their emotional status, to*
> *discriminate among these motions and to use this*
> *information to guide thinking and actions. (Salovey*
> *& Mayer 1990, p. 187)*

Understanding emotions and the emotional temperament of others is necessary to determine how particular emotional abilities are used in decision contexts as well as specific work-related settings.

Increasing a personal focus on EI provides an opportunity to realise it as a significant factor in assisting people in the process of positioning and repositioning that is negotiating and navigating through complexity, not only about other people but also about themselves. Having decided on a career, most people come to their roles highly motivated.

This chapter also focusses on a variety of models to consider, learn and develop. Careers do not follow a linear route and require creative discovery and development. For people facing persistent change, adapting to change assists them to their align career goals with those of the organisation's. However, career thinking is not only cognitively based but also emotionally based.

Emotional Stamina

For some time now, interest in EI and its influence on action has increased. A person's ability to identify and process emotions, theirs and others, and use their emotional capability to their advantage. Improved understanding of multiple intelligences includes two key domains: 'intrapsychic' and 'interpersonal skills' (Gardner, 1983). Gardner's introspective contributions to EI development provided an opportunity to introduce theoretical frameworks describing management philosophy and the leadership paradigm. Theorists assert that EI is the capability to examine and censor one's own and others emotions, to differentiate among separate emotions and to employ information to handle thinking and actions (Mayer, Salovey, & Caruso, 2008).

Emotional Categories		Cognitive Capabilities
Perceptions	(a)	Identify emotions especially contradictory ones
	(b)	What are appropriate/inappropriate emotions in a given situation?
	(c)	Understand how emotions are displayed based on context and culture
	(d)	How do you learn to express emotions accurately?
	(e)	Understand emotions through observing nonverbal behaviour
	(f)	Understanding emotions through the prism of one's temperament
Emotions facilitating thinking	(a)	Identify issues that are triggered by emotions
	(b)	Leverage mood to generate different cognitive perspectives
	(c)	Prioritise thinking by directing attention according to present feeling
	(d)	Trigger feelings to understand the experiences of another person
	(e)	Activate feelings in assessing a situation
Understanding emotions	(a)	Cultural diversity
	(b)	Empathy
	(c)	Emotional transitions
	(d)	Complex and mixed emotions
	(e)	Emotional triggers
	(f)	Background factors
	(g)	Emotional interrelationships

Emotional Categories	Cognitive Capabilities	
Managing emotions	(a)	Others' emotions
	(b)	Own emotions
	(c)	Maintain, reduce or intensify and emotional response
	(d)	Understand emotional reactions
	(e)	Tap into emotions to gain an effective outcome
	(f)	Recognise positive and negative emotions

It is essential to follow a planned approach to considering career options, which includes explorative. It is a three-pronged approach, which includes the following:

(1) purpose,

(2) perspectives, and

(3) outcomes.

CAREER PURPOSE

Career decision making is a complex process that involves harmonising work-related factors such as the location of work, working conditions as well as personal factors such as 'fit' and proximity to home. Former work experiences are important in careers decision making.

Exploration

An interactive, intention-oriented approach changes depending on where people are, whom people are with, what time it is and what people want from any given situation. Interactions with people's families are different from interactions with their colleagues. These changes of behaviour are the result of different 'intentions' people hold within different groups or between individuals. Become aware of how these intentions and tactics affect people in their career choice.

(1) What do they *want* or *need*? What are they striving for or struggling to achieve? What are their goals?

(2) What are the *obstacles*?

(3) What *tactics* will they use to overcome any given obstacle? Tactics allow fully invested choices to be explored.

(4) What will it specifically *look like* when the person has succeeded? What will they see, hear, taste, touch and smell so they know they are on a suitable career track?

(5) Answers need to be intuitive and compelling based on the person's goals and perceived barriers.

Connecting emotions, cognitions and action is an effective way of exploring career motivations. Careers are not cloaks to put on and take off; they are fully personified and lived.

(1) Developing an intuitive GOAL.

(2) Overcoming substantial OBSTACLES.

(3) Employing a variety of TACTICS.

(4) Imagining the EXPECTATION of success.

Career thinking and making is not too dissimilar from entrepreneurial thinking. Both are focussed on opportunity-seeking strategies and focus on 'how, by whom, and with what effects opportunities create how careers are forged through discovered, evaluated, and exploited' (Timmons & Spinelli, 2004, p. 101).

Questions to assist this process are as follows:

1. What do they know about this career?

2. Why? This is an essential question as it goes to the heart of motivation and aspirations.

3. What do they perceive as career outcomes?

4. How?

5. What is involved?

6. Who will they become in this career?

7. When will this happen?

8. Where are they heading now?

CAREER AMBITION

Ambition is a universal need for the attainment of some kind (Hogan & Chamorro-Premuzic, 2015; Judge & Kammeyer-Mueller, 2012); for example, to write a best-selling novel, to work for the homeless, to start up a business or to become a prime minister. Often, ambition indicates to others an ardent, even ruthless craving for advantage. For that reason, it is frequently distrusted, especially in certain spheres, for example, politics, sales, as it is seen primarily as self-interested (Judge & Kammeyer-Mueller, 2012). Whether now or in the past, most cultures are imbued with a negative sense of ambition being typified, for example, by self-interest.

'In every place, ambition and avarice penetrate …'. (Machiavelli, 1965, pp. 11–12)

For this reason, people do not always declare their ambition and sometimes either downplay it or avoid it for various reasons, for example, deliberately avoiding promotion, for the fear of being seen as overly ambitious due to its unpleasant overtones (Hogan & Chamorro-Premuzic, 2015).

And yet, ambition or at least, aspiration, is central to career thinking and a person's life story and to understand how it is directed, and shaped into something constructive. This sentiment of accepting and managing career goals rather than seeking to diminish them is acute. Volunteering is an example of a person's ambition to contribute to something beyond themselves, which also has a self-interested aspect, for example, new learning, enjoying working with others, derive self-satisfaction when giving to others. Ambition is either inert, emergent or distinct and this, in turn, is shaped by external factors such as career trajectories, institutional, occupational and work design parameters, relationships with others as well as personal experiences and self-perceptions.

Career development is still seen as serving time, and so an ambitious person cannot be seen to be 'getting ahead of themselves' (in other words, 'getting ahead of others'). With this in mind, there are two issues to consider: first, 'getting ahead of others' is hierarchical depicting power and control. People, who have achieved this status through their ambition, have more social influence than others, adopt a sense of self-importance and superiority, and if so have heightened self-esteem and which in turn influences how others perceive or trust them. Some people actively avoid seeking promotion for these reasons if nothing else, to minimise their distress about negative perceptions of 'getting ahead of others'. The second reason is to consider why in the past and even today, there are so few women and minorities represented in the top echelons of their societies. It is important to note that people with ambitions require external support in some form, for example, mentoring, being given an opportunity, access to training and development.

Getting ahead of oneself (tantamount to control) and getting along with others are the 'the two big problems' in managing career ambition (Hogan & Roberts, 2004, p. 209). The attributes of effective leadership, having aspired and gained it, is to gain acceptance by 'bringing others along with you'. Control, getting ahead and getting along with others are serious for lowering everyone's anxiety (including the incumbent) about the leader (Baumeister, 2005).

Despite the potentially negative perceptions about ambitious people, whether self-declared or not, they are more likely to present positively; engage and achieve well in all spheres and reap the associated rewards, money, status and respect (Judge & Kammeyer-Mueller, 2012). Further, ambitious people achieve these outcomes by planning and setting goals for their future, aimed at achieving success (Elchardus & Smits, 2008). Some people are actively interested towards autonomy and competence, while others are driven by extrinsic factors such as remuneration and benefits (Ashby & Schoon, 2010), and outward success such as status (Judge & Kammeyer-Mueller, 2012).

People with ambition are more likely to be focussed on goal and career, owning their career and taking the initiative as well as doing more than is expected (Barrick et al., 2013) ultimately leading to satisfaction and career success (De Vos & Soens, 2008; Forret & Dougherty, 2004). Ambition, and even exhibiting enthusiasm rather than spurning or masking it, is linked to levels of remuneration and benefits (Chng & Wang, 2015).

Employers, educators and those in the career development industry need to recognise ambition and how people are socialised either to pursue it or not. Part of the problem lies in managers and others not knowing how to manage ambitious people especially if the opportunities for advancement are not there, or worse, feeling threatened by them and either shunning or bullying them out of the organisation or other strategies to thwart their attempts to achieve their goals. Managers often refer to Gen Y staff wanting to step into positions without going through the time honoured (institutionalised) steps to reach them. If ambition is thwarted, people will seek alternative options.

In summary, being ambitious means that people are more likely to be motivated to succeed not only extrinsically but also intrinsically and this changes over time. Ambition is not self-ignorance about one's capability or confidence.

CAREER SUCCESS

Achievement and failure are ideological symbols of careers, both leading to blind spots and so people become 'stuck' in careers or bounded by conventional thinking. In both cases, people hold on to past judgement and experiences (theirs or others) and do not lean into the future. Careers are the stories people tell about ourselves and others use to tell about them.

Achievements accumulated in the course of working are perceived as career success (Seibert, Kraimer, & Liden, 2001). In the past, success was often evaluated by external factors such as income, position title and a rapid progression through the career hierarchy (Judge, Cable, Boudreau, & Bretz, 1995). By contrast, intrinsic factors of career success include personal perceptions such as achievements and career satisfaction (Barrick, Mount, & Judge, 2001).

Consequently, the factors that contribute most to career success depend on the context, timing and how individuals use these to their advantage. In other words, when referring to career success, it is probably more apt to see to it as career potential, such as the capacity for technical skill, creative aptitude and so on. Potential ability and fit for a role develops over time, stimulated and qualified by the interaction between factors external to the workplace as well as internal to it. A person's self-appraisal is needed in both assessing career success and likewise, career failure.

CAREER FAILURE

Most people strive to appear capable to others, especially at work, and others work hard managing the impression of being successful. Failure takes many forms including personal missteps or incidents that occur outside a person's control, for example, a work accident. Often, the person is blamed or victimised in regard to the latter. Managing impressions of being successful or not failing require concealing information from others about personal failures such as poor decisions or miscalculations. However, it is not always possible to conceal personal failure associated with careers.

How people experience and reflect on failure is essential to understand. One way of thinking about failure is an outcome that leads to unexpected or unintended outcomes. Using this perspective permits the person or group to learn from the experience rather than dismiss it out of hand.

As discussed above, self-reflective practice conducted positively assists a person to understand what works well and what areas they need to improve, which helps shapes future goals, both personal and career. High ambition and negative self-reflection can induce overly harsh self-appraisal having an adverse outcome (Mongrain & Zuroff, 1995). This negativity can, in turn, lead to poor goal-progress, across a variety of domains and an over pre-occupation with potential failure (Powers, Milyavskaya, & Koestner, 2012). If this is the case, independent feedback (i.e. apart from self-reflection) needs to be sought (Hattie & Timperley, 2007), and essential for tracking goal-progress. Unless this occurs, people set themselves up for future failure.

People do not know the future; however, they need to engage in tacking towards it in a similar way to sailing on a yacht. Tacking means the boat keeps going whether the wind is supporting it or not, and if the latter, tacking is about turning the boat around to find a new course where the wind will help it advance. Sometimes, people lose momentum in their career journey, and they need to try a different approach or a new course of action. Even in periods of inertia, a person is planning their next move.

Understanding whether a career is changing course, changing tack or being influenced by other factors is necessary to recognise. Framing the situation is important for making plans and decisions. For example, questions such as: what is the risk of making an incorrect decision; if the risk is high, what will be the impact; and what is the risk if a decision is not made?

Once a decision is made, the flaw, often self-imposed for whatever reason, is not delivering on it. For these situations, people need to develop an action plan. As indicated above, ambition and success are tightly linked but more often than not, ambitious people, who are achievement-orientated, experience failure. Their arduous drive often protects them by providing resilience to overcome these setbacks. Consequently, performance and outcomes result in multiple combinations of success and failure, including partial, immediate versus complete and gradual; ongoing or not. Failure is more conspicuous than success because, especially in media and social media age, negative information has more currency than 'good news' story (Pinker, 2018).

Similarly, people single out their failures, and in spite of this, they focus on the emotional outcome of the experience rather than potential learning gained from letdowns. By contrast, failure is a focus in some very specific cases, for example, life and death occupations, sports, construction projects and similar cases where there are tangible links between participants' contributions and outcomes. Disappointments in these contexts lead to learning opportunities as people need to modify their actions to improve performance (Sitkin & Pablo, 1992). In sport or any physical performance such as playing a musical instrument, contributing factors to failure are more readily identifiable, which, in turn, is the stimulus to learn from the experience.

By comparison, occupations or pursuits, which are less challenging physically although more complex socially, tend not to address failures in any meaningful way at least, for those people engaged in them. In these settings, people lean towards accrediting accomplishment to effort, motivation and capability, and accrediting failure to factors which lie outside a person's control (Jones & Harris, 1967). Conversely, people also, at times, assign others' successes to external causes and others' failures to internal causes and de-motivate those involved to learn from their experience (Diwas, Staats, & Gino, 2013). In some cases, to do so might lead to industrial relations or legal matters between the parties. Consequently, people either ignore learning from failure, engage in cover up or self-protective emotion.

As a general rule, people initially do not respond well to failure in most situations, particularly in a career context as it involves a person's identity, which is fractured or tarnished irrevocably, particularly if the failure becomes widely publicised. For example, people will cover up, become cautious, moderate their performance and goals, and, at times, retaliate if they see others are responsible for their failure. Much of this distress is turned inward (Clark & Thompson, 2013; Dweck, 2008). As well as the individuals who fail, most organisations are ill-equipped to deal with the failure of their staff or their business. How people respond in a career crisis is indicative of their emotional control and that of their work culture. Failure is often linked with inferior outcomes, low skill and individual incompetence rather than being an outcome of poor structures, policies or the inevitability of striving to perform differently. While it is possible to minimise failure in the sense of always playing it safe, it would result in a dull, uninteresting life (Norman, 2013).

Failure is a complex phenomenon as it involves not only individual but also wider structural issues. Making errors or failing is a reality in everyday life and provides a significant learning opportunity if it is recognised and reflected upon. Notwithstanding that errors and failures are challenging, any analysis and response are risky and emotionally fraught. For example, receiving feedback about poor performance is difficult for most people to accept.

Similar to success, failure for one person is not necessarily relevant for another person as there will be situational or contingencies that will also contribute to the outcome.

Types of Failure

Failures and errors cut across expected and favoured intentions (Zhao & Olivera, 2006). There are failures when people break the rules, errors such as lack of capability, poor application of skill, insufficient knowledge or making an incorrect decision (Lei, Naveh, & Novikov, 2016).

Like success, the experience of failure is steeped in emotions. How people manage their emotions at the time of failure is important for insightful reflection. As stated above, people will learn if they reflect on failure (Epstude & Roese, 2008). The outcomes of error and failure learning include changes in understanding (Argote, 2012), actions (Shepherd, Patzelt, & Wolfe, 2011) or performance improvement (Zhao, 2011). Nevertheless, not all errors and mistakes fail. From time to time, making a mistake results in the better outcome such as when it leads to a new idea, new learning or new connection. Constructive learning following an error comes from understanding mistakes or failure and more importantly, how to respond to it.

Motivation to Learn through Experienced Failure

Supporting people through failure is precarious for a positive and healthy outcome. The way people perceive and respond to failure is also related to their coping strategies. Assisting people to understand this and how this impacts different outcomes associated with failure provides significant learning and coping. Further, the more committed people are to their organisation and career, the more likely this lessens the negative responses to failure (Shepherd et al., 2011). The inter-relationship between high career commitment and failure is weakened when people remain strong in coping with negative outcomes arising from disappointment. Negative emotions also decline when people see failure as inevitable (Shepherd et al., 2011).

Regardless of its nature, emotions are expedient in assisting people in learning from setbacks they experience. Beliefs about failure that see it as inevitable are inculcated learning for both participants and bystanders as it guides future actions and encourages people to take risks at work without fear of reprisal. Personal disappointment is an inescapable part of life. Despite this, failure is often considered worthless. For example, investigating notions of regret has demonstrated that when peoples lip-up, they engage in undesirable actions such as avoiding otherwise good choice strategies (Ratner & Herbst, 2005) or contesting feedback that is subsequently beneficial (Reb & Connolly, 2009).

Emotive and cognitive responses are expected responses to letdowns. Letting both cognitions and emotions emerge following a less-than-good performance or outcomes serves to promote (demote) investing further effort in either the task at hand or the organisation. Even the anticipation of a future failure leads to poor choice by making it difficult for people to come to a solution. Often, failure is regarded as a setback (Bandura, 1991), and leads to self-doubt and giving up (Crowe & Higgins, 1997), and sometimes, labelling themselves as a failure (Bandura, 1991).

Although unpleasant and sometimes dysfunctional, failure at times is useful in avoiding future mistakes (Saffrey, Summerville, & Roese, 2008). People learn through socialisation to develop different coping strategies for dealing with failure and not have it define or impede them (Dweck, 1986). For example, people improve their performance when they have learnt or, in fact, repeated work where they had failed in the past (Brunstein & Gollwitzer, 1996) if the experienced failure facilitated learning through self or facilitated reflection. With this in mind, failure and the subsequent meaningful action to overcome it, and repeated error making, become complex. A sense of balance between success and failure, especially for young people, is required.

After making a mistake, people will employ a variety of coping strategies, anything from denial to trying again to see if they can improve on their last performance. When experiencing failure, some people try to work out how to improve or the reasons for failure and recognise how they can recover from this experience on subsequent occasions (e.g. cognitions that aid performance and learning, Epstude & Roese, 2008). These types of thoughts occur when people realise that learning from the initial mistake is valuable or when they reflect (Epstude & Roese, 2008).

Managing negative feelings involves changing the way failure is perceived so that people can cope and feel better about themselves. These are termed 'self-protecting strategies and includes post-hoc rationalisation, where people rise above the failure and move on quickly from it as the consequences are moderated' (Patrick, Lancellotti, & de Mello, 2009). Failures also are externalised, or the consequences downplayed (Zeelenberg & Pieters, 2007).

An emotional focus might lead appreciatively to dissimilar conclusions. Attending to adverse emotions associated with past failures often motivates people to do better next time. Whether this eventuates or not depends on what they learnt from their experience and how they used it to improve on it in subsequent situations (Adolphs, Tranel, Damasio, & Damasio, 1994). When someone faces an emotional response to a situation, they remember both the experience as well as how they felt about it. If they come upon a similar situation sometime later, this memory is activated (Baumeister, Vohs, DeWall, & Zhang, 2007). The undesirable emotions post-failure stimulate people to recover from their errors in ensuing episodes. However, this memory is not triggered every time as it largely depends on the extent to which the person can identify similarities between the past and current situation in which they find themselves (Baumeister et al., 2007).

People who assess their mistakes following errors are actively searching for a method not to repeat them. Although recalling negative feelings about mistakes is important, the real focus needs to be on the goal and the intended outcome in similar, subsequent situations. People learn best when they receive appropriate information following a letdown and have the time to assimilate it. The event itself is valuable if people take the time to examine its consequences (Argote, 2012).

A successful recovery from failure rests on the frequency and recency of events.

CAREER THINKING PERSPECTIVES

Developing Reflective Practice for Career Thinking

Reflective practice is a method to address these questions and requires discerning both current and past responses knowledge to produce newly interpreted understandings. Comprehension is at the centre of reflective practice and includes both cognitive and emotional perspectives to ascertain significant influences in specific situations, contradictions, that is, which factors are discrete and which ones are interrelated. This discernment is a vital part of career thinking and making.

Maintaining momentum through self-reflection is powerful (Madrigal, Gill, & Willse, 2017). As people strive to understand the meaning of competitive outcomes, failure attributions play an important role in future psychological performance states by influencing emotional stamina.

Being self-aware is important for emotional stamina (Cowden, 2017) and how the attributions that people employ following a failure are important cognitions underlying emotional stamina (Meggs, Ditzfield, & Golby, 2014). Believing in oneself is also essential, and focussing on positive elements of failure are important (Madrigal et al., 2017).

The reflective practice is conducted as suggested above or used in conjunction with a framework (based on Barbulescu, 2017) as outlined as follows. It is important for people at a career transition point to:

(a) focus on relevant experience;

(b) interrogate the experience; and

(c) the reason why and how they acted, interacted and responded, critiquing it from another person's viewpoint (based on Harrison & Lee, 2011).

Taking each one in turn:

(a) Focus on relevant experience, such as:

- identifying previous personal experiences, situations, experiences or relevant professional practices could be a source of learning;

- becoming aware of repeated experiences that demonstrate beliefs and conceptions about oneself and others; and

- evaluating beliefs and conceptions about oneself and others.

(b) Interrogating the experience

- inquiring and focussing: investigating possible actions by formulating questions and hypotheses about the context and one's response.

(c) Examining the reasons about why and how they acted, interacted and responded and critiquing it from another person's viewpoint (based on Harrison & Lee, 2011)

- planning objectives and future actions to initiate a new reflective cycle, and

- explaining the change of direction.

A career is not a given; it is a process of emergence which, at this current time, is in a state of flux, as indicated in Fig. 1. Some careers are well-established, steeped in an occupational heritage over a long period while others are emerging or yet to be spawned. Most career transition and develop over

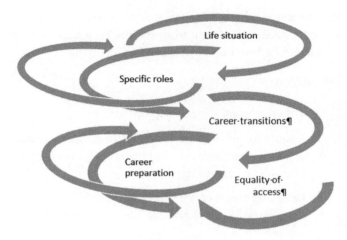

Fig. 1.   Career Thinking Frames.

time, while others are fleeting and short-lived. Some careers
are highly technical and technologically dependent, which is
more so today than ever before.

Careers are considered from several perspectives: macro,
micro, objective, subjective based on bureaucratic abstrac-
tions of organisational experience or immersed and localised.
Diverse perspectives inform the career exploration process,
particularly the 'why' question: the reasons underlying the
intention and purpose.

Although the notion of a career for life will be less true
for future generations, careers still require some degree of life
cycle thinking and frequent re-thinking. How people engage
in this process is fundamental.

As technology and society continue to evolve, organisations are responding by transitioning to more flexible structures, work and roles bringing with it change in workforce
capability moving towards project work requiring teams.

Careers are shaped by scientific, social and economic inter-
developments. Career thinking is at a cross road, that is, a

disconnect between employment and career support provided by employers and how universities, schools, career counsellors support career entrants. The high unemployment in certain skill areas, for example, points to this critical junction. Decisions and developments in the past have a long-lasting effect on institutional arrangements as well as career thinking by major stakeholders, which requires a fundamental shift of career analysis from *ex post* to *ex ante*.

How should people think about the future, and more importantly, how do people's assumptions underpin their thinking about careers at a time of the paramount uncertainty and the need to reinvent or develop? Developing a conceptual map with a career as the dominant focus and allowing themes to emerge is an initial starting point. It is important not to limit the notion of career to how it was used in the past or present. Careers develop either through innovation or stagnation.

> *Getting hold of the difficult deep down is ... Hard ... because if it is grasped near the surface, it simply remains near the surface, it simply remains the difficulty it was. It has to be pulled out by the roots, and that involves people's beginning to think about these things in a new way. The change is as decisive as, for example, that from the alchemical to the chemical way of thinking. The new way of thinking is what is hard to establish. (Wittgenstein, 1946, p. 48)*

Rethinking career assumptions does not mean forsaking all past aspects, just those that are less viable.

> *Reality is that which is expected to reveal itself indeterminately in the future. Hence an explicit statement is on reality only by virtue of the tacit coefficient associated with it. ... If explicit rules*

can operate only by virtue of a tacit coefficient,
the ideal of exactitude has to be abandoned. What
power of knowing can take its place? The power
which people exercise in the act of perception. The
capacity of scientists to perceive the presence of
lasting shapes as a token of reality in nature differs
from the capacity of people's ordinary perception
only by the fact that it can integrate shapes presented
to it in terms which the perception of ordinary
people cannot readily handle. (Polanyi, 1967, p. 10)

Career thinking is based on either a pictorial construction or narrative construction by people within everyday conversations about careers that convey values about their future career motivations, for example, innovation, risk-taking, personal control and active development of one's skills and career in a rapidly changing highly uncertain labour market (Peter & Bröckling, 2016). People also compose narratives when interviewing for a job, during a performance review, when networking, with co-people complaining about their supervisor in the tea room, an inventor describing their 'ah-ha' moment, the owner of a start-up or as a person wanting to gain a loan from the bank or complaining about poor service. In terms of the former, most people are intrigued by these stories, for example, *TedX* is based on this phenomenon. People can also 'flip the script', learning to perform the institutionally required narrative (Carr, 2011) to demonstrate a different side of themselves.

When asked to reflect on the past, most people end up telling a story, created by memories and imagination. These stories represent a '…structural force that affects people's life-chances and as an ideology of governance that shapes subjectivities' (Ganti, 2014, p. 90). The narrative, whether life or incident, is a way of positioning identity and capability.

These accounts tend to place the narrator at the centre of the situation and how they overcome some difficulty, which was blocking them from achieving what they wanted. For example, an unfairly dismissed employee might relate how triumph came when they started up their own business and now earn more money than ever before and perhaps gloat over the news that their former employer is now out of business due to the market downturn.

Life stories of 'successful' career incumbents often encompass a career prototype including the experience of travails, how they found meaning and purpose through their struggles. Other stories are told by people who have dedicated themselves to their communities, expressing a strong commitment through volunteering to the well-being of future generations either through community service, or political involvement. Narratives either expressed online or in person, frequently suggest an alternative career model and thinking.

What these stories show is that career making is fluid and often emerges out of specific situations. People perceive that they do not have enough information to know what, when, why, where and how future careers will unfold. Their only guide is to draw a line from today – using the present as a foundation. It is important to reflect on these situations to maximise career thinking and learn by diagnosing the process of defining a vision and setting direction, intervening in others or careers being disrupted by others; as well as through exercising influence over other people and organisations and community through volunteering. Whatever the case, career is transformational for everyone as people need to make sense of what is going on, bestow meaning and purpose as well as learn to cope with and evaluated the challenges.

More analytically, perhaps it is the phenomenon of temporal discounting. People often prevaricate about acting towards their careers as they succumb to the present's more pressing issues, assuming that time is on their side including planning for their retirement (e.g. Munnell, Webb, & Golub-Sass, 2009), exercising or studying (e.g. Oyserman, 2015).

The way people think about careers is also found in various philosophical perspectives. As previously stated, '..... from the alchemical to the chemical way of thinking' (Wittgenstein, 1946, p. 48). To find a new way of thinking involves reflecting phil-osophically by employing different perspectives and using the principles and assumptions of each to challenge the others. For example, the naturalist tradition sees nature as the organising principle, including the human mind. People take into account the ever-present environment, which poses limits and opportuni-ties. Epistemologically, the rationalist views thinking and reason-ing as separate from nature. However, there is symmetry between thinking and sensing, one influencing the other, whereby the per-son acts responsibly and ethically. People construct their social world and include unresolved and un-resolvable tensions and contradictions. There is not one simple solution to such matters.

There is no right answer or one solution. Career is not an equation that adds up or is simply optimisable. Some things are complex, or they meet conflicting assumptions, so that simple solutions are not available.

What is new is a sense that the twenty-first century requires distinctly new capabilities – cognitive, affective, creative and technical – and that K-12 and higher education institutions need to be radically re-made or 'disrupted'. This change is required to manage realistically the changes confronting young people confronting career choice and development.

ACTION-ORIENTATED AND GUIDED LEARNING

Two different processes will convert experiences into better performance outcomes, such as action-orientated learning and guided learning. Action-orientated learning is mostly unconscious and implicit. Guided learning, on the other hand, involves dynamic questioning and choice making, where a coach or mentor together with the incumbent draws out information about a prior event to form commitments about how to change things in the future (Thomson, Turner, & Nietfeld, 2012). It is imperative that learning from failure is linked to future choices.

Time

Time is an important dimension in career thinking. Time spent in paid and unpaid work, in learning activities includes: paid work (all jobs); job search; attendance of classes at all levels of instruction (pre-primary, primary, secondary, technical and vocational, higher education, extra or make up classes); research/homework; travel to and from work/study; other paid work or study-related activities.

Time spent in unpaid work includes routine housework; shopping; care for household members; child care; adult care; care for non-household members; volunteering; travel related to household activities; other unpaid activities.

Autonomy

The autonomy of thinking is important too. It provides the mental and operational space that allows individuals to prioritise their tasks, freeing up the time that they need to learn from failures (Kerr, 2009).

Coping Strategies

There are three types of coping orientations: loss, restoration and oscillation. Shepherd et al. (2011) analysed how these orientations affect learning. Loss orientation refers to the explicit processing of a failure to break the emotion that is associated with the failure (a failed project). Restoration orientation refers to suppressing feelings of loss and instead proactively focussing on the tasks that arise as a consequence of the failure rather than preventing future failures. An oscillation orientation refers to moving back and forth between loss and restoration orientations. Individuals who have stronger loss and oscillation orientations report a better ability to learn from previous project failure than those with a restoration orientation. The necessary element is the capacity to disconnect from the failure, particularly from an emotional perspective, which suggests that effective learning involves managing the emotions evoked by a failure.

Emotional Response

A person's capacity to recover from successes and failures is shaped by how strongly they feel about it. To strengthen positive emotional responses such as resilience and deal with the highs and lows of career outcomes requires emotional resilience bolstered by support from others. Only then can people learn and reflect positively on what worked and what did not and the reasons for this.

Positive Learning Relationships

Positive relationships gained through mentoring and coaching, whether formal or informal, not only encourage emotional well-being but also boost information processing and coordination capacity, which, in turn, have positive effects on the capacity to learn from failure (Carmeli and Gittell, 2009).

Creative Self

Creativity is the making of novel and applicable ideas about products, practices, services or procedures (Tierney & Farmer, 2011). It emanates from a defined 'self-belief that one can produce creative outcomes' (Tierney & Farmer, 2002, p. 1138). Being creative is important for successful outcomes and dealing with failure. Both require resilience and grit or in other words, persistence. Emotional stamina is urgent for finding purpose (Gucciardi, 2017) as are problem solving strategies (Nicholls, Gaynor, Shafiei, Bosanac, & Farrell, 2011) and self-belief (Chen & Cheesman, 2013).

In today's uncertain world of work, employment is both flexible and individualised 'contracts' are used to maximise the potential of skill and aptitude (Atkinson & Sandiford, 2015). Job security is weakening both due to uncertainty, remote working, individualisation and, subsequently, decline in union membership resulting in less uniform employment and benefits (Rousseau, Hornung, & Kim, 2009).

The explanations that people give for causes of events along this dimension have been shown to have implications for, self-efficacy (Bond, Biddle, & Ntoumanis, 2001) and confidence (Parkes & Mallett, 2011); both of which are components of emotional stamina.

Emotional stamina is valuable to explore how it predicts specific patterns of attributions (Golby & Sheard, 2006). There are differences in emotional stamina and controllability cognitions following failure between genders. For example, Crust and Swann (2013) reported higher levels of sense of control for men compared to women.

360 Degree Thinking

Using as many perspectives as possible to embark on a process of self-discovery is important. Human understanding comes from being in touch with personal values to appraise a potential alignment with the values of a prospective career and employer.

The following is a simple set of questions to assist with self-reflection:

(a) How imaginative do you regard yourself?

(b) In considering options for problem solving and decision making, do you methodically collect information to support your views?

(c) How ready are you to evaluate your assumptions?

(d) How open are you to consider new ideas?

(e) How well to you weigh up the pros and cons of expected outcome(s) of your decisions?

(f) How tolerant are you with experiencing uncertainty?

(g) How well do you plan and prioritise your time when considering a career change?

(h) How ready do you action a decision outcome?

Thinking In-Contradiction

People augment their views by investigating and expanding their or other's counter-opinions as well as other diverse understandings when considering their own experience. A person considers how they feel about career options from a less emotional perspective. Innovators also frequently apply this approach to developing ideas. This method establishes a quasi-ambivalence about choices and choice sets.

Despite the value in creative and inherently conflictual thinking, a comprehensive contradiction is a potent stance from which to work through various standpoints. Intrapersonal conflict emerges when taken-for-granted assumptions are questioned, particularly about career notions. Despite the value of reframing, people find it difficult to think outside their normal frames. There is a benefit in there is value in vigorously looking for, identifying and communicating ideas that oppose or else challenge people's primary arguments, nonetheless provide helpful discernments. A thinking-in-contradiction approach offers a more rounded perception of career experiences, first, second or third-hand.

One way to manage this is to quarantine the immediately un-resolvable and put it to the side for future interrogation. Cognitive dissonance (Festinger, 1957), a form of uncertainty, offers a basis for handling the contradictions by way of nuancing them. Uncertainty is a lack of predictability about future conditions and mirrors understanding, in that reducing uncertainty leads to an increase in comprehension. First, it magnifies what is relevant to a choice, taking more things into account when considering a problem. The next step is to investigate multifaceted interrelationships, emphasising key overlaps. At this stage, the challenge is viewed in its totality, focussing on purpose rather than the components of the issue. Potential compromises are acted upon. Combining ideas leads to a more creative solution than discounting them.

Decision making is never purely rational. People make choices based on beliefs, stereotypes, biases, interests and experiences which are rarely evidence based, open to change, often stated with authority and misleading. The process of collecting evidence for decision making is coloured by these too. People agree with those who seemingly support what they know and rely on and disagree with those who do not. People are more likely to focus on poor choices than positive ones. People also expect others to agree with and support them in their decision making. People learn and trust those things that are tangible.

Control in Choice Making about Careers

Focussing on controlling outcomes is a barrier to making good choices. Hence, people who vacillate about career choice making are more positive than they seem. Career uncertainty is inevitable. Fostering a skill set to manage ambiguity is important not only to augment career choices but also generally in life.

Personal Disruption: Readiness to Overcome Career Adversity

Personal disruption includes the perception of the disconnection itself and its consequences for the individual as well as others, both in the present and in the future. At the point of experiencing consequences, people need to reflect how prepared they were for the change: did they see it coming? If so, did they prepare for it or avoid it? How will they adjust to future changes? These questions will be addressed next. What learning will take place once the disruption has occurred? This latter question will be discussed in the latter half of the chapter.

People who are flexible and adaptable are usually highly valued in the workplace, especially at the time of disruption. Equally, in career development and change, people who possess these capabilities are investing in their working life longevity. When opportunities are identified, those who adjust to the new circumstances, for example, by reinventing themselves is a good insurance policy for the future, short and long term. This approach is not too dissimilar to any investment by perceiving what is at stake means that people will bypass a short call and opt to take advantage of the opportunity, thereby underlying a more secure future, longer term. A perspective with a longer horizon permits people to identify opportunities or downturns and in that way, position themselves to withstand disruptions.

Resilience or flexibility is the ability to deal with challenges, including failure. Some have referred to it as the capability to understand, deal and at times, endure change as it occurs, whereas career adjustment is more proactive (Bimrose & Hearne, 2012). Forward-thinking people seek out information channels to search and mine data sources to assist them and, thus, are more likely to sense career opportunities and disruptions earlier than others. Equally, flexible people see obstacles as a challenge to deal with rather than something to avoid. In that sense, failures are regarded as learning opportunities. People with a learning mindset are less likely to be daunted when fronting trials.

Similarly, people who doubt their capabilities do not position themselves well for the future. When people doubt their capability, they sometimes feel undeserving of what they have achieved. This feeling is underpinned by disbelief about their success, despite others acknowledging their skills and accomplishments. The reason for raising it in this context is that it can curb people from pursuing further opportunities and curtail their career goals and development.

INTERPERSONAL ASPECTS OF CAREERS

From a psychosocial viewpoint, social networks are defined as 'digital spaces' allowing users to manage both their network of social relationships (organisation, extension, exploration and comparison) and their social identity (description and definition). Moreover, social networks allow the creation of amalgam of social networks, leading to a new social space, more flexible and dynamic than earlier social networks.

Social Skills

The cognitive and emotional outcomes of people building interactions are absorbed through such interpersonal relations and are maximised through cultural diversity. Cultural collaborations such as co-existence and fusion of diverse ideas activate innovative outcomes.

Real-time personal interaction is vital in working relationships, including those online to activate this process. The development of social skills, collaboration, influence skills, networking and sharing of practices are all essential for both generating and executing new ideas (Poysa-Tarhonnen, Elen, & Tarhonnen, 2016). Networking is decisive for innovation, both in developing ideas at any point in a person's career trajectory (Morris, Webb, Fu, & Singhal, 2013; Pache and Chowdhury, 2012). The disruption of conventional thinking by cultural engagement and understanding facilitates new thinking.

Building Trust: A Key to Collaboration

Collaboration demands mutual trust and integrative thinking (discussed further in Chapter 4). Trust develops through frequent and expressive interactions, where individuals disclose openly without fearing reproach from others.

Trust helps establish a climate of support and encourages self-disclosure and sharing feelings. Virtual collaboration is exceedingly demanding as it takes time to adjust to new ways of working. Understanding factors that will influence people's vulnerability is important as it is the initial phase for career planning, taking into account contingencies at the pre-career stage as well as during and post-appointment related changes that people need to withstand. For example, a role description cannot fully depict what lies ahead and besides, it changes over time.

Empathy

Empathy is a salient element of social cognition that contributes to a person's capacity to understand and respond to the emotions of others, to communicate passionately and to share with others (Spreng, McKinnon Mar, & Levine, 2009). There is a distinction between the cognitive and emotional components of empathy (Rankin, Kramer, & Miller, 2005). Although it is difficult to ascertain what aspects of empathy are associated with perspective taking, sympathy, personal distress, emotional contagion or insight are needed for an empathic response (Spreng et al., 2009).

Empathy is needed to gain insight into how others are feeling and requires skills in active listening, curious conversations and relationship awareness. It is a process when another person perceives that another person is feeling something very similar to what they are feeling (based on Hoffman, 2000).

This process is depicted in Fig. 2, which shows that empathy involves some form of cognitive and emotional states (e.g. guilt), identified by both the perceiver and the perceived. For example, when a person walking down a

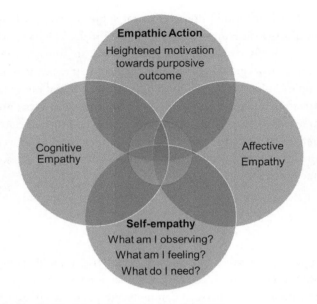

Fig. 2.   A Model of the Empathy Process.

street encounters a homeless person requesting a monetary donation, what form of empathy is the passer-by feeling? Cognitive empathy means that the passer-by feels that the homeless person is hungry, cold, etc., versus the homeless person triggering those actual feelings in the passer-by. The more familiar people are with each other's situations, the more likely they will feel responsible for responding in some effective way. Empathy, how people feel and express it, varies according to experience.

Affective empathy occurs when people react rapidly in situations that they 'feel at one with'. People, who are aware of the situation or emotions of another, are more likely to be aroused emotionally or will engage in more perspective taking, and will exhibit more empathy than someone who does not. Both forms, that is, cognitive and affective empathy, are important for self-empathy, and all three contribute to empathic action.

Producing Outcomes

Consistently following through on their commitments and delivering on outcomes is essential for maintaining a career. It requires a strong action plan for this to occur. It is important to establish realistic goals and timelines too. People need to align their expectations of themselves against this. This approach points to a person's organisation and planning capability.

WELL-BEING AND CAREER CHANGE

A career shift, whenever it occurs (i.e. mid-career or otherwise), represents either a point where a person undergoes a separation from one career to the next or an inflection point in a specific career trajectory. Changing their career midstream often requires the need for people to reinvent themselves and bring their knowledge from one career domain to another. Career shifts reflect changes of interest or disruption of some kind in the workplace. A person may exit their existing occupation and move into another industry, occupation or both. More often than not, these shifts are inflection points, markers of a change of direction within a continuous career stream.

Leadership changes and the inevitable restructuring of organisations and work that follows disrupt people's careers, often with little preparation. Change under these conditions leads to a degree of discomfort, exacerbated for those with a low-risk appetite for change. Career framing and envisioning future change is essential. As stated earlier, learning and knowledge are the basis of career thinking. Knowledge is social, and so is learning. Both are derived from doing, experimenting and experiencing, for example, theories-in-action (Argyris & Schön, 1974) and so as all people are learners.

People assume that education, training, development and experience are ideal ways for considering the various dimensions and decision points for a future career. Are these forms of preparation applicable, given the heightened uncertainty and disruption? While thinking and preparing for the future puts people in the driving seat of change, making choices and in doing so, shaping it not only for themselves but also others and in so doing harnessing complexity as a skill rather than a conundrum.

Learning occurs best in practice. Consequently, learning processes that stimulate and galvanise embedded knowledge (tacit knowledge) and develop it further by exposing to both social deliberations and interrogations. Discussion and learning build a capacity to cope with the future, including reflection on action (Johnsen, 2012).

Tacit Knowledge

Tacit knowledge and expertise are important issues. For example, the use of metaphors indicates tacit knowledge in the workplace (Sternberg & Horvath, 1999). Tacit knowledge emerges through learning in practice as well as workplace conversations and forms the basis for coping, developing and thinking about people's future. Co-learning not only focusses on the workplace but also on global challenges (Gustavsen, Hansson, & Qvale, 2008).

Given the disruption and the likely future outcomes, it is important to rethink careers from a learner's perspective, such as co-learning rather than a trickle-down approach from the top echelons of institutions – focussing on the assets and strengths of learners; developing resources to support and build upon their learning assets; nurturing ownership of personal career development; and building entrepreneurial networks that increase the competitiveness and impact of these efforts. Career and choice making go hand-in-hand and shape the kind of careers that people will inevitably lead including their family and social life. These more personal spheres of life need to be factored into the career equation. The family is a significant contributor towards developing expectations as well as a person's peers, teachers and significant processes such as work-integrated learning, internships and other forms of work experience (e.g. a family business).

As people label themselves through socialisation and are pigeon-holed by others, this categorisation typically contributes to their interests, values, goals and ultimately, career choices. Prospective career entrants explore the plethora of information about career fields and choices. This exploration is matched by the divergence of the originators of such information to enhance decision making about careers and career pathways.

This process improves the ability of people to sense and make-sense of novelty, including the richness of ephemeral time-space unique phenomena; and second, that this enhanced ability to appreciate, even cultivate complexity, for instance as 'ontological expansion' (Tuomi, 2017), facilitates people adopting strategies intended to improve their prospects for resilience and a more balanced approach between designing, creative spontaneity as well as risk taking.

CONCLUSION

The foundation of this book is on co-learning, that is, a learner-driven approach to innovation, a way for people to shape their thinking to achieve a career outcome. Co-learning is actively engaging participants and encouraging them to converse together and partner in their reflections. This type of thinking, which is collective and social, is contrasted with a more individualised conventional approaches, where formal academic inputs have been prioritised. Most importantly, collective learning helps people to cope with the future.

One of the clear benefits of co-learning is commencing the learning journey from people's everyday experience, whether that is their work, university or school environment. Significant depth and creation emerge through the co-learning process and in particular through the engagement of people at different stages of their career, working together as peers. In being exposed to the co-learning process, the participant draws upon diverse forms of thinking and method to canvass career options and ultimately a career prototype as outlined in Chapter 5. A career prototype includes (a) goals, (b) relevant tasks, (c) prospective interactions, (e) task interdependencies and (f) outcomes.

Co-learning careers is not easy as it means letting go of *a priori* assumptions and involves active listening to the 'different' perspectives of others while simultaneously attempting to understand each person's reality as different but complementary to others. It takes a lot of time to prepare and facilitate sessions and requires facilitators to always have the bigger picture in mind. At times, it is tempting to fall back to prescribing 'these are the steps in implementing change' or 'these are the components to develop careers'. It involves a challenge to move out of one's 'comfort zone'. It is culturally sustaining learning, whereby career strategies are relevant to the experiences and practices of people, especially young people transitioning from school to work and minority groups. These strategies need to both develop and sustain people, too (Paris, 2012).

Finally, it is notable that a number of generic issues emerge such as thinking about a career beyond being of intrinsic or instrumental value. It involves affective, cognitive and experiential learning all important for developing a growth mindset. For example, co-learning is action-orientated, encouraging the participant to think beyond the insular towards a capacious, universal questioning and understanding.

REFERENCES

Adair, W. L., & Loewenstein, J. (2013). Talking it through: Communication sequences in negotiation. In M. Olekalns & W. L. Adair (Eds.) *Handbook of research on negotiation*. (pp. 311–331). Cheltenham: Edward Elgar.

Adolphs, R., Tranel, D., Damasio, H., & Damasio, A. (1994). Impaired recognition of emotion in facial expressions following bilateral damage to the human amygdala. *Nature 372*(6507), 669–672.

Ang, S., Van Dyne, L., Koh, C., Ng, K-Y., Templer, K., Tay, C., & Chandrasekar, N. A. (2007). Cultural intelligence: Its measurement and effects on cultural judgment and decision making, cultural adaptation and task performance. *Management and Organisation Review, 3*, 335–371.

Argote, L. (2012). Organisational learning research: Past, present and future. *Development and Learning in Organisations: An International Journal, 26*(2), 320–321.

Argyris, C., & Schön, D. (1974). *Theory in practice: Increasing professional effectiveness.* San Francisco, CA: Jossey-Bass.

Ashby, J., & Schoon, L. (2010). Career success: The role of teenage career aspirations, ambition value and gender in predicting adult social status and earnings. *Journal of Vocational Behaviour, 77*(3), 350–360.

Atkinson, C., & Sandiford, P. (2015). An exploration of older worker flexible working arrangements in smaller firms. *Human Resource Management Journal, 26,* 12–28.

Bandura, A. (1991). Social cognitive theory of self-regulation. *Organisational Behaviour and Human Decision Processes, 50*(2), 248–287.

Barbulescu, A. (2017). Modelling the impact of the human activity, behaviour and decisions on the environment. Marketing and green consumer (Special Issue). *Journal of Environmental Management, 204*(3), 813–813.

Barrick, M. R., Mount, M. K., & Judge, T. A. (2001). Personality and performance at the beginning of the new millennium: What do we know and where do we go next? *International Journal of Selection and Assessment, 9,* 9–30.

Baumeister, R. F. (2005). *The cultural animal.* New York, NY: Oxford University Press.

Baumeister, R. F., Vohs, K. D., Nathan D. C., & Liqing, Z. (2007). How emotion shapes behaviour: Feedback, anticipation, and reflection, rather than direct causation. *Personality and Social Psychology Review, 11*(2), 167–203.

Bimrose, J., & Hearne, L. (2012). Resilience and career adaptability: Qualitative studies of adult career counselling. *Journal of Vocational Behaviour, 81*(3), 338–344.

Bond, K. A., Biddle, S. J. H., & Ntoumanis, N. (2001). Self-efficacy and causal attribution in female golfers. *International Journal of Sport Psychology, 32*(3), 243–256.

Brunstein, J. C., & Gollwitzer, P. M. (1996). Effects of failure on subsequent performance: The importance of self-defining goals. *Journal of Personality and Social Psychology, 70*(2), 395–407.

Carmeli, A., & Gittell, J. H. (2009). High-quality relationships, psychological safety, and learning from failures in work organisations. *Journal of Organisational Behaviour, 30,* 709–729.

Carr. (2011). Emotional stamina. In *Scripting addiction: The politics of therapeutic talk and American sobriety*. Princeton, NJ: Princeton University Press.

Chen, M. A., & Cheesman, D. J. (2013). Mental toughness of mixed martial arts athletes at different levels of competition. *Perceptual and Motor Skills, 116*(3), 905–917.

Chng, D. H. M., & Wang, J. C. Y. (2015). An experimental study of the interaction effects of incentive compensation, career ambition, and task attention on Chinese managers' strategic risk behaviour. *Journal of Organisational Behaviour, 37,* 719–737.

Clark, A. M., & Thompson, D. (2013). Successful failure: Good for the self and science. *Journal of Advanced Nursing, 69*(10), 2145–2147.

Cowden, R. G. (2017). On the mental toughness of self-aware athletes: Evidence from competitive tennis players. *South African Journal of Science, 113*(1–2), 6–6.

Crust, L., & Swann, C. (2013). The relationship between mental toughness and dispositional flow. *European Journal of Sport Science*, *13*(2), 215–220.

De Vos, A., & Soens, N. (2008). Protean attitude and career success: The mediating role of self-management. *Journal of Vocational Behaviour*, *73*(3), 449–456.

Dewey, J. (1933). In J. A. Boydston (Ed.), *Essays and how we think revised edition in the later works of John Dewey* (*Vol. 8*). Carbondale, IL: Southern Illinois University Press.

Dewey, J. (1941). Propositions, warranted assertibility, and truth. In L. A. Hickman & T. M. Alexander (Eds.), *The essential Dewey volume two: Ethics logic psychology* (2nd ed., pp. 201–212). Bloomington, IN: Indiana University Press.

Diwas, K. C., Staats, B., & Gino, F. (2013). Learning from my success and from others' failure: Evidence from minimally invasive cardiac surgery. *Management Science*, *59*(11), 2435–2449.

Druckman, D., & Olekalns, M. (2013). Motivational primes, trust and negotiators' reactions to crisis. *Journal of Conflict Resolution*, *57*, 959–983.

Druckman, D., Olekalns, M., & Smith, P. (2009). Interpretive filters: Social cognition and the impact of turning points in negotiation. *Negotiation Journal*, *25*, 13–40.

Dweck, C. (2008). *Mindset: The new psychology of success*. New York, NY: Ballantine Books.

Earley, P. (2003). *Cultural intelligence: Individual interactions across cultures*. Stanford, CA: Stanford University Press.

Elchardus, M., & Smits, W. (2008). The vanishing flexible: Ambition, self-realisation and flexibility in the career perspectives of young Belgian adults. *Work, Employment and Society*, 22(2), 243–262.

Epstude, K., & Roese, N. J. (2008, May). The functional theory of counterfactual thinking. *Personality and Social Psychology Review*, 12(2), 168–192.

Festinger, L. (1957). *A theory of cognitive dissonance*. Stanford, CA: Stanford University Press.

Foronda, C., Baptiste, D. L., Reinholdt, M. M., & Ousman, K. (2016). Cultural humility: A concept analysis. *Journal of Transcultural Nursing*, 27(3), 210–217.

Forret, M. L., & Dougherty, T. W. (2004). Networking behaviours and career outcomes: Differences for men and women? *Journal of Organisational Behaviour*, 25, 419–437.

Ganti, T. (2014). Neoliberalism. *Annual Review Anthropology*, 43, 89–104.

Gardner, H. (1983). *Frames of mind: The theory of multiple intelligences*. New York, NY: Basic Books.

Giele, J., & Elder, G. (1998). Life course research development of a field. In J. Giele & G. Elder (Eds.), *Methods of life course research: Qualitative and quantitative approaches* (pp. 5–28). Thousand Oaks, NJ: Sage Publications.

Glaser, B. G. (2001). *The grounded theory perspective: Conceptualization contrasted with description*. Mill Valley, CA: Sociology Press.

Golby, J., & Sheard, M. (2006). The relationship between genotype and positive psychological development in national-level swimmers. *European Psychologist, 11*(2), 143–148.

Gustavsen, B., Hansson, A., & Qvale, T. U. (2008). Action research and the challenge of scope. In P. Reason, & H. Bradbury (Eds.), *The Sage handbook of action research, participative inquiry and practice* (pp. 63–76). London: Sage.

Harrison, J. K., & Lee, R. (2011). Exploring the use of critical incident analysis and the professional learning conversation in an initial teacher education program. *Journal of Education for Teaching: International Research and Pedagogy, 37*, 199–217.

Hattie, J., & Timperley, H. (2007). The power of feedback. *Review of Educational Research, 77*(1), 81–112.

Hermans, H. J. M. (2013). A multi-voiced and dialogical self and the challenge of social power in a globalizing world. In R. W. Tafarodi (Ed.), *Subjectivity in the twenty-first century. Psychological, sociological, and political perspectives* (pp. 41–65). Cambridge: Cambridge University Press.

Hoffman, M. L. (2000). *Empathy and moral development: Implications for caring and justice.* Cambridge: Cambridge University Press.

Hogan, R., & Roberts, B. W. (2004). A socio-analytic model of maturity. *Journal of Career Assessment, 12,* 207–217.

Johnsen, H. L. (2012). Making learning visible with ePortfolios: Coupling the right pedagogy with the right technology. *International Journal of ePortfolio, 2*(2), 139–148.

Judge, T. A., Cable, D. M., Boudreau, J. W., & Bretz, R. D. (1995). An empirical investigation of the predictors of executive career success. *Personnel Psychology*, *48*(3), 485–519.

Judge, T. A., & Kammeyer-Mueller, J. D. (2012). On the value of aiming high: The causes and consequences of ambition. *Journal of Applied Psychology*, *97*(4), 758–775.

Kerr, A. (2009). A problem shared ... ? Teamwork, autonomy and error in assisted conception. *Medicine*, *69*(12), 1741–1749.

Lei, Z., Naveh, E., & Novikov, Z. (2016). Errors in organisations: An integrative review via level of analysis, temporal dynamism, and priority lenses. *Journal of Management*, *42*(5), 1315–1343.

Machiavelli, N. (1965). In A. Gilbert (Trans.), *The chief works and others*. Durham, NC: Duke University Press.

Madrigal, L., Gill, D., & Willse, J. (2017). Gender and the relationships among mental toughness, hardiness, optimism and coping in collegiate athletics: A structural equation modelling approach. *Journal of Sport Behaviour*, *40*(1), 68–86.

Mayer, J. D., Salovey, P., & Caruso, D. R. (2008). Emotional intelligence: New ability or eclectic traits? *American Psychologist*. *63*(6), 503–517.

Meggs, J., Ditzfield, C., & Golby, J. (2014). Self-concept organisation and mental toughness in sport. *Journal of Sports Sciences*, *32*(2), 101–109.

Mongrain, M., & Zuroff, D. C. (1995). Motivational and affective correlates of dependency and self-criticism. *Personality and Individual Differences*, *18*(3), 347–354.

Morris, M. H., Webb, J. W., Fu, J., & Singhal, S. (2013).
A competency-based perspective on entrepreneurship
education: Conceptual and empirical insights. *Journal of
Small Business Management, 51*(3), 352–369.

Munnell, A. H., Webb, A., & Golub-Sass, F. N. (2007). *Is
there really a retirement savings crisis? An NRRI analysis
(Issue Brief No. 7–11)*. Chestnut Hill, MA: Centre for
Retirement Research, Boston College.

Nicholls, D., Gaynor, N., Shafiei, T., Bosanac, P., &
Farrell, G. (2011). Mental health nursing in emergency
departments: The case for a nurse practitioner role. *Journal
of Clinical Nursing, 20*(3–4), 530–536.

Norman, D. A. (2013). *The design of everyday things*. New
York, NY: Basic Books.

Oyserman, D. (2015). *Pathways to success through identity-
based motivation*. New York, NY: Oxford University Press.

Pache, A. C., & Chowdhury, I. (2012). Social entrepreneurs
as institutionally embedded entrepreneurs: Toward a new
model of social entrepreneurship education. *Academy of
Management Learning & Education, 11*(3), 494–510.

Paris, D. (2012). Culturally sustaining pedagogy: A needed
change in stance, terminology, and practice. *Educational
Researcher, 41*(3), 93–97.

Parkes, J. F., & Mallett, C. J. (2011). Developing mental
toughness: Attributional style retraining in rugby. *The Sport
Psychologist, 25*, 269–287.

Patrick, V., Lancellotti, M., & de Mello, G. E., (2009).
Coping with non-purchase: Managing the stress of
inaction regret. *Journal of Consumer Psychology, 19*(3),
462–473.

Peter, T., & Bröckling, U. (2016). Equality and excellence. Hegemonic discourses of economisation within the German education system. *International Studies in Sociology of Education*, *26*(3), 231–247.

Pinker, S. (2018). *Enlightenment now: The case for reason, science, humanism, and progress*. New York, NY: Viking Penguin Random House, LLC.

Powers, T. A., Milyavskaya, M., & Koestner R. (2012). Mediating the effects of self-criticism and self-oriented perfectionism on goal pursuit. *Personality and Individual Differences*, *52*(7), 765–770.

Poysa-Tarhonnen, J., Elen, J., & Tarhonnen, P. (2016). Student teams' development over time: Tracing the relationship between the quality of communication and teams' performance. *Higher Education Research & Development*, *35*, 787–799.

Rankin, K. P, Kramer, J. H., & Miller, B. L. (2005). Patterns of cognitive and emotional empathy in frontotemporal lobar degeneration. *Cognitive Behavioural Neurology*, *18*(1), 28–36.

Ratner, R. K., & Herbst, K. C. (2005). When good decisions have bad outcomes: The impact of affect on switching behaviour. *Organisational Behaviour and Human Decision Processes*, *96*(1), 23–37.

Reb, J., & Connolly, T. (2009). Myopic regret avoidance: Feedback avoidance and learning in repeated decision making. *Organizational Behaviour and Human Decision Processes*, *109*(2), 182–189.

Rousseau, D. M., Hornung, S., & Kim, T. G. (2009). Idiosyncratic deals: Testing propositions on timing, content, and the employment relationships. *Journal of Vocational Behaviour*, *74*, 338–348.

Saffrey, C., Summerville, A., & Roese, N. (2008). Praise for regret: People value regret above other negative emotions. *Motivation and Emotion*, *32*(1), 46–54.

Seibert, S. E., Kraimer, M. L., & Liden, R. C. (2001). A social capital theory of career success. *Academy of Management Journal*, *44*(2), 219–237.

Shepherd, D. A., Patzelt, H., & Wolfe, M. (2011). Moving forward from project failure: Negative emotions, affective commitment, and learning from the experience. *Academy of Management Journal*, *54*(6), 1229–1259.

Sitkin, S. B., & Pablo, A. L. (1992). Reconceptualising the determinants of risk behaviour. *Academy of Management Review*, *17*(1), 9–38.

Spreng R. N., McKinnon M. C., Mar, R. A., & Levine B. (2009). The Toronto empathy questionnaire: Scale development and initial validation of a factor-analytic solution to multiple empathy measures. *Journal of Personality Assessment*. *91*(1), 62–71.

Sternberg, R. J., & Horvath, J. A. (Eds.) (1999). Tacit knowledge in professional practice. In *Researcher and practitioner perspectives*. Mahwah, NJ: Lawrence Erlbaum Ass.

Thomson, M. M., Turner, J. E., & Nietfeld, J. L. (2012). A typological approach to investigate the teaching career decision: Motivations and beliefs about teaching of prospective teacher candidates. *Teaching and Teacher Education: An International Journal of Research and Studies*, *28*(3), 324–335.

Tierney, P., & Farmer, S. M. (2002). Creative self-efficacy: Its potential antecedents and relationship to creative performance. *Academy of Management Journal, 45*(6) 1137–1148.

Tierney, P., & Farmer, S. M. (2011). Creative self-efficacy development and creative performance over time. *Journal of Applied Psychology, 96*(2), 277–293.

Timmons, J. A., & Spinelli, S. (2004). *New venture creation: Entrepreneurship for the 21st century*. Chicago, IL: Irwin Press.

Tuomi, I. (2017). Ontological expansion. In R. Poli (Ed.), *Handbook of anticipation* (pp. 1–35). Cham, Switzerland: Springer International Publishing.

Wittgenstein, L. (1970). *Culture and value*. London: Blackwell.

Zeelenberg, M., & Pieters, R. (2007). A theory of regret regulation 1.0. *Journal of Consumer Psychology, 17*(1), 3–18.

Zhang, G., Zeller, N., Griffith, R., Metcalf, D., Williams, J., Shea, C. & Misulis, K. (2011). Using the context, input, process, and product evaluation model (CIPP) as a comprehensive framework to guide the planning, implementation, and assessment of service-learning programs. *Journal of Higher Education Outreach and Engagement, 15*(4), 57–84.

Zhao, B., & Olivera, F. (2006). Error reporting in organisations. *Academy of Management Review, 31*(4), 1012–1030.

PART II

STRATEGISING CAREERS

3

CAREER STRATEGISING

INTRODUCTION

The twenty-first century has spawned deep vicissitudes in the labour market, making it more complex for individuals to acclimatise to work and decide on career directions (Savickas, 2015). As global change gathers momentum, people are concerned about their career opportunities, universally and personally. Uncertainty is characteristic of the career terrain rendering some groups and some people, especially low-skilled people, at higher risk than skilled people (Masdonati & Fournier, 2015).

Uncertainty is fundamental for career strategising. It is taking a 'wide angle' view of the world of opportunities. More significantly, it is the ability to act creatively, that is, to be open to possibilities and acquire a healthy risk appetite under these circumstances is also prudent. This stance opens people up to creative problem solving and trying to understand if there is a problem and if so, what and why is it.

As stated in Chapter 1, work configures not only people's experience at work but also in the community as well as at home. People also shape work and jobs, some of which are idiosyncratic to them. In most cases, role incumbents shape their work to suit themselves as much as their employer. Sometimes, this shaping is done intentionally and sometimes not as it just evolves. In other cases, an employer identifies a person who seems to have the talent they want at the time and offers them a role. Increasingly, the demands of customers, clients or technology are configuring work in terms of the nature of the tasks, requiring a renegotiation of task or role boundaries (Cruz & Meisenbach, 2018) or change in cognitive emphasis. This type of evolution of work is not a recent phenomenon; however, the realisation and application of this are apposite for career strategising.

Part I of this book focusses on the meaning and transformation of careers for people today. Part II develops some of the key ideas and opens up disruptive growth. Disruptive development focusses on new opportunities such as transitioning from one career to another or creating career opportunities that have not previously existed.

Strategising entails at a minimum, four processes:

(1) taking into account relevant evidence associated with the issue;

(2) understanding objective and subjective responses to the evidence;

(3) committing to develop a path of future action; and

(4) embarking on a passage of personal change – tomorrow's self.

CAREER CHOICE, TRANSITION AND DESIGN

There are a handful of significant decisions that a person makes in their life time, which are considered demanding. Career decision making is one of them as it impacts a person's life noticeably. Even if the person engages in it for a relatively short period, it changes the course of their life. Because of this, career choice is hard as people weigh up the benefits versus the costs.

Creating Choices or Designing Choices

When confronting a new challenge, people often reach for what has held them in good stead from their past experience. Perhaps, instead of reaching for the tried and faithful method, consider if it is time to become more creative in thinking to canvass tomorrow's options. As an alternative of journeying down the career path alone, contemplate joining with others, for example, peers, current employees working in areas of interests, to assist in weighing up what works or not as well as what are the benefits and loses.

Decision Making

Understanding the actions of people in career making is fascinating. For example, in choosing one option, people reject other alternatives. Why? People's choices are influenced by both their emotions and cognitions, often treated independently, although usually privileging logic and rationality over emotion. For example, decision making is considered logical, relying on factual evidence, generating pros and cons, analysing the impact of each and ultimately selecting the best alternative. Typically, decision making is viewed not only as logical but also bounded by rationality (Simon, 1956) and includes the following processes, which are iterative and not undeviating:

(a) Assume that the career problem is solvable.

(b) Define it clearly, devoid of emotion.

(c) Diagnose the situation to ascertain the contributing factors.

(d) Identify the possibilities to deal with the problem.

(e) Prioritise the options based on a pro–con evaluation.

(f) Make a decision.

(g) Set a timeline to action.

(h) Monitor and review.

(i) Bring into play a contingency plan, if the timeline becomes over-stretched.

Other types of decision making, which are interconnected, include the following:

(a) Assimilating or accommodating to make new decisions (Piaget, 1955).

(b) Thinking differently.

(c) Muddling through (incrementalism) (Lindblom, 2010).

(d) Sense making (Weick 1995).

(e) Adjusting to changes.

Seeing decision-making in this way is not representative of how people make choices (Barnard, 1938) — for example, making life decisions, whether it about buying a house, car or choosing a career, is essentially skewed based on a person's knowledge, experience as well as their feelings and past actions (Simon & Newell, 1958). Decision making is shaped by experience and cultural learning (values, assumptions and beliefs) as well as emotions and form a circuit with one aspect triggering another (Epstein, 1994). Decision making about careers is also a dynamic process and the option selected, from a range of best and worst case scenarios, is the one that makes sense at the time for a given context to bring about a satisfactory outcome.

Career making, accordingly, engages people in various ways. A career is material, in the sense that it affords a degree of utility, security and opportunity for the incumbents and their dependents. It similarly has an emotional basis that shapes how people work and engage with others at work, all of which shape subsequent career choices. Career is also symbolical in how it represents and signifies status, rewards, power and privileges. The material, emotional and symbolic elements of career shape preferences including a:

(a) physical preference for the work, for example, hours of work, work times, work place, distance, quantity or quality of work;

(b) social preference includes co-workers, networks;

(c) psychological preference associated with the brand or reputation identity of the employer, personal interests and needs; and

(d) normative preference for an alignment of personal values with occupational or employer ones such as caring for the environment, and religious beliefs.

Cognitions and emotions shape how people respond and make choices for themselves now and in the future. Career design focusses on emotions which are complex to quantify (Masdonati & Fournier, 2015; Nota, Ginevra, & Santilli, 2015). People conceive time and space suggesting a capacity to see beyond the current (Kant in Onora, 1975). Similarly, the capacity of people to develop reasonable knowledge about what they experience is based on both insight into matters and the ability to recognise the different nature of things as well as being able to have a perceptive reflection and social deliberation.

Designing an idiosyncratic career is both opportunistic for the incumbent and the employer given its adaptive value. Storytelling is an effective tool for critical thinking. Through narration, the person indicates a view of self now and in the future (Savickas, 2015). Through storytelling, people can reflect on themselves more objectively, especially if they narrate vocally to others, highlight and indeed, pinpointing noteworthy facets of their experiences. People gain insights into how their experiences shaped their conundrum, permitting them to design a positive intervention for change. Encouraging people to consider their strengths is also important as it enables them to attend to poignant emotions, preferences and actions in developing choice options (Ferrari, Sgaramella, & Soresi, 2015).

Strategising a career is essential for crafting an overarching career goal, initiated by the following questions:

(a) What is the main goal to be acted upon? For example, is it to manage, supervise, organise, co-ordinate, deliver, operate, design, serve, teach, invest, train, etc.?

(b) What needs to be mobilised, for example, people, projects, finances, information other resources?

(c) To what end?

(d) In what setting, for example, a large corporation, NFP, fieldwork, classroom, health facility, etc.?

A career strategy aims to bundle opportunities, repackage them to form a novel choice set or invent a new one. Most inventors garner ideas from a pre-existing pathway of discovery. Innovation relies on picking up the threads of what has gone before and continuing that trajectory to take it in a new direction by viewing the problem or the solution differently. It is through this process that innovative careers emerge.

Whatever a person's career strategy is, designing a portfolio of options for possible directions is an effective way of considering the future. A career portfolio is an investment portfolio. It needs to be well-balanced with an appropriate risk threshold to reap a strong return on both personal and resource investment.

CAREER PROBLEM SOLVING

Problems are encountered in everyday living and vary in complexity and type (accessible through step-by-step analysis, e.g. system breakdown; inaccessible through a step-by-step approach, e.g. career choice; or a combination of these). Different strategies are used to solve these problems, including experience, tacit knowledge and skill, calling on others to assist (Weller, Villejoubert, & Vallée-Tourangeau, 2011). Solving problems is often not straightforward, requiring muddling through (trial and error) as well as creative insight. The outcome of problem solving is multilinear, highly unpredictable and sporadic. Both forms of problem solving involve elements of insight and reflection to a greater or lesser extent (Kounios & Beeman, 2014).

Problem solving or productive thinking (Hurson, 2008) is beneficial for career thinking as new ideas and discovery thinking are needed. 'The more change you face, the more you need productive thinking' (Hurson, 2008, p. 49). It uses both creative thinking and critical thinking.

How do people go about solving problems? A conventional approach focusses on how people 'think' and so the emphasis is often on how to improve thinking. An effective problem solving framework contains the following iterative phases: (a) problem-finding; (b) knowledge acquisition; (c) information-gathering; (d) incubation; (e) idea generation;

(f) idea-combining; (g) selection of best ideas; and (h) externalisation of the ideas (Sawer, 2012).

The alternative approach focusses on how people 'see and listen' and ways to improve these functions – that is, to discover, develop and exploit an opportunity. Knowledge is a key resource not only in the hyper-globalised world of today but also for career making. In any situation, a person's knowledge is limited by their past and present experiences, their networks of relationships and, most importantly, their view of the future. One way is to analyse and solve problems through a blend of both convergent and divergent thinking outlined as part of design thinking a career in Chapter 4. In this chapter, the focus is on the processes underlying career decision making.

Career Decision Making

Career choices are tough and often life-changing in every sense (family, life-style, financial, leisure time, etc.). Labour markets expand or contract the latitude of career choice. Where choice is severely restricted, it often leads to depleting a person's value rather than augmenting it. For career strategising, a person needs to know something about specific careers, for example, requirements, demands, expectations of others about those careers.

Career decision making is complex; at times, opportunistic, and context specific (Lindblom1979, 2010). Being decisive is a career-enhancing skill in itself, especially in the context of ambiguity, piecemeal facts and in novel situations. Making a decision is superior to not making one, even if the decision turns out not to go as well as expected (Weber, Baehr, & Wells, 2002).

Different kinds of knowledge and knowing come from different sources. The truth about the universe is different from the truth about a person's perceptions of their experiences. How can people, based on these reflections and references, know something about the future? Their knowledge is based on what they learn from direct experience and stakeholders. Despite any former requisite knowledge, making rational decisions is challenging. Perceptions and interpretations of reality get in the way. It is from this 'muddle' that people learn. As a result, individual rationality and objectivity are acknowledged and also contribute to a person's reality. It is vital to reconcile different aspects of accumulating and assimilating. Creating scenarios assists this integrative process and is outlined below in this chapter.

WHY STRATEGISE A CAREER?

Strategising is a form of interrogation, which assumes a relationship between theory and practice in career making. Replacing career planning and strategising inform career choice, design and outcomes in different ways that will be teased out in this chapter. However, as anyone knows who has engaged in career planning, this relationship is problematic. Strategists typically work in broad areas and are principally practitioners, not theorists as it focusses on the future and its likely outcomes in specific domains. Several key factors are associated with this demand, including the:

(a) disruption of economic change;

(b) latent knowledge and skills;

(c) capability adjust to future changes; and

(d) failure to perceive opportunities in change, present or future.

Strategising is also intended to forge or alter an existing or new career direction, combining personal intent coupled with situational intent. To be effective, people need to feel a degree of comfort with uncertainty as this approach is future-orientated and extrapolative. What the future holds is unknown. Values and expectations fill in the gaps when evidence is limited. This shapes the form and nature of strategising and the influence of values on people's interpretation of their future.

People who engage in career strategising rely on internalised premises, tacit and often unexamined. There is never one single or best career solution for an incumbent; there are many. People have opportunities to make an impact, and creative thinking and strategising assist them in this quest to formulate and consider some of the options. Scenario designing promotes the designer to interrogate these, not to take them for granted and even to share them to render them more explicit.

Career strategising is based on 'theories-in-use' (Arygris & Schön, 1974) to imagine what 'might be'; what form career trajectories and practices might take. In doing so, they not only refresh existing assumptions based on new information, question current career frameworks but also develop career thinking capability which facilitates hypothesising, 'scenario-ising' and choice making. Discovery is precipitated by process of questioning using direct questions, closed questions, open questions and tentative questions directed by self or other.

A strategy has three parts:

1. a diagnosis of a conundrum involving a choice that the person is striving to surmount;

2. a guiding philosophy in the shadow of potential choices and a formulation intent of coherent action that is followed through to bring about the choice; and

3.   shaped by values, uniqueness and ethics is a great
      strength for forging a career commitment as well as high
      cognitive intelligence and high emotional intelligence to
      enable resilience and overcome future career setbacks.

Questioning

Questioning is a key part of a strategist's tool kit. It is a practical conduit to discovery, especially during disruptive innovation (Dyer, Gregersen, & Christensen, 2011). Success in most
careers, regardless of disciplinary knowledge, is achieved
through questioning (Mattimore, 2012, p. 31), whether this
pertains to the incumbent's work directly or indirectly to their
career. Questions propel participants into discovering new
ideas. Addressing questions brings people closer to choice and
decision making. In other words, scoping questions is invalu-
able in isolating the central issues that spark creativity.

Metaphors

Societal and cultural ways of understanding are epitomised
by metaphors. They are situation relevant and embody social
and cultural processes of understanding and meaning. Finding new metaphors to reflect career realities is easier said
than done as they are embedded in the everyday language
of life (Dweck, 1996). To communicate metaphors effectively
requires creative ways of communication; for example, 'any
utterance, phrase, or word whose meaning varies with the
context in which it is produced in a way that could not be pre-
dicted from the lexicalised meanings of its component words'
(Gerrig & Gibbs, 1988, p. 2). People employ creative imagery
when they encounter new experiences, often finding it difficult to convey the meaning to others. Experiential learning

is part of this process. It is gaining knowledge, skill and awareness, which is directed into career thinking. This process is expedited by reflective journaling so that participants integrate reflection, action, feeling and thinking (Gerrig & Gibbs, 1988).

In a fast-paced world, probable social, political, economic and technological fluctuations shape choices, decisions and outcomes. Attitudes are internalised. The creative process occurs largely subconsciously. While people's subliminal aspirations are best suited to drawing novel connections, it is also guided by their emotions (Solomon, 1993). If a person is reticent about their creative know-how, they are stymied and worse still, not aware that this is happening. Considering problems deeply and valuing novelty for its own sake is incisive for triggering creative processes (Sternberg, 2014).

There is a relative absence of understanding of this overarching perspective among non-expert participants with people attending to individual and personal preferences rather than the structural, social or cultural determinants of careers. The career focus pinpoints the individual with increasing inattention to the wider context shaping work and work organisations. Such a disregard limits thinking about careers as something that is shaped by systemic factors and is amenable to change. Bringing a deeper appreciation of the systemic forces to career thinking is vital to learn how social, political and technological factors shape careers.

It is salient to promote how contextual factors contribute to the development of career, or lack thereof warrants a mediation strategy. Improved recognition of the social dimensions of the issue opens the prospect for policy and practice amendment to address future careers and pathways. Improving public understanding is not only important for people seeking careers but also for shedding light on the issue and calling for structural change.

People need a better understanding of the causes, consequences and possible solutions to career finding. When people acknowledge the role of wider societal factors that are at play in career issues, for example, a wider range of policy and practice solutions becomes visible and is seen as appropriate and effective.

Communicating the choices made, how information is presented, including explicit and implicit messaging is powerful in how people understand an issue and the solutions they support (Nyhan & Reifler, 2010). People are sometimes unaware of the forces that shape careers and career pathways is one factor why they identify a narrow range of career options for themselves, which is potentially self-limiting. In addition, when making career choices, people generally have a lack of awareness about the breadth and application of their capability for a greater diversity or future careers. Conversely, they are less restrictive when suggesting career options for others.

Using metaphors is one way for people to tackle these blind spots and raise their awareness to learn about the systemic determinants of careers and potential pathways and more pertinently, how to intercede in this process. Employing metaphors is a process for spawning information among stakeholders and simultaneously promoting a more robust discussion about careers and career development.

Using metaphors is one method of framing or contextualising issues (Lakoff & Johnson, 2003). In this capacity, metaphors help to translate new information or knowledge in terms of what is known (Chiappe, Kennedy, & Smykowski, 2003). By using metaphors, facilitators assist people to think and talk productively about complex and unfamiliar issues in more proficient and informed ways (Thibodeau & Boroditsky, 2011). Metaphor is a process of projection of an understanding of one situation on another, hence the term. In addition to questioning, employing the use of metaphor allows people to simplify something complex, either cognitively or affectively to make sense of it (Vosniadou & Ortony, 1989). It has several functions:

(a) prompts information processing and knowledge;

(b) signifies a rounded grasp of knowledge gained; and

(c) mirrors societal and cultural ways of understanding (Moser, Clases, & Wehner, 2000).

Metaphorical framing, in summary, progresses understanding of a range of issues and the connections among them. This method serves to amend or append new ideas to routine patterns of thinking that normally preclude people from seeing the importance of contexts, systems and policies in solving career problems (Kendall-Taylor et al., 2014a). In widening understandings of how issues work, framing them is likely to lead to a more creative consideration of factors, drive rigorous debate of diverse approaches and increase support for solutions (Kendall-Taylor et al., 2014b). Issue framing creates support for evidence-based strategies and, in turn, assists in reforming approaches to better address career demands.

Information Processing

Metaphors not only enable the reflection and communication of complex topics but also the anticipation of new situations. The use of diverse metaphor models affects further insight, explanation of practices and frequently, subsequent actions (Gentner & Gentner, 1983). Metaphors have not only influential importance for self-reflection, anticipation and communication but also an important function as mind settings, which influence people's cognition of the self and the world around them (Ottati, Rhoads, & Graesser, 1999).

Understanding and Knowledge

Metaphors are an example of a distributed representation of complex knowledge and analogical problem solving. For example, a career is often depicted as a journey or a pathway to life, with the novice taking steps towards the ultimate goal of an expert. This metaphor resonated at an earlier time for people and needs to be replaced to reflect the complexity of the world of work and working.

Metaphors in Use

There are types of creative skill arising to implement metaphorical analysis: synthetic skills to draw new connections, the analytical skills to separate good from bad ideas and the persuasive skills to overcome the resistance to novelty. Synthetic skills are developed through the practices outlined above, and the remaining two will be addressed below.

A career strategy incorporates the choice to decide what is 'ruled' in and what is out. A selected career domain area (SCD) is a space, a capacity or both, which a person intends to pursue (Fig. 1).

Ingenuity is needed for strategising both long-term and short-term ones. What connects one to the other are the tactical decisions made as an interim step towards attaining a longer-term goal. The timeframe for SCD is about 5 years. As stated earlier, risk and uncertainty are key factors in determining career strategies. Any options open for investing in a career strategy is influenced by varying levels of risk and uncertainty. Readiness to make strategic choices amid uncertainty has been counted among the sine qua non prerequisites for people to gain a foothold in a dynamic labour market.

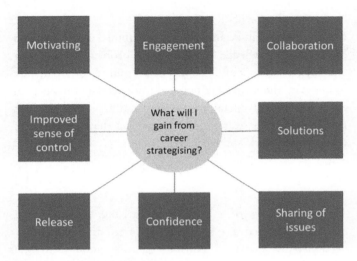

Fig. 1. Career Strategising.

Imagination

Imagination is the mode by which people relate to something non-existing or unknowable. Moreover, relating to the future is possible only through imagination, and this imagination always has a creative component.

What makes it possible for people to relate to something non-existent is imagination (Sartre, 2012). While people's senses and perception connect them to something they understand, memory connects them to the given (and, in this sense, existing) past. Imagination is a form of consciousness by which people relate to what does not exist, including the future. This process is important for both strategising and prototyping, discussed in Chapters 4 and 5.

Sartre points out that imagining an object is a way of relating to the object itself. The image is just a means to relate to the existing or non-existing object. Sartre (2012) calls the image an analogon of the object, a perception of pictures and models 'animated' by people's imaginations. When people read a novel, their interpretation is coloured by their imagination. The text becomes an analogon in the same way as a wire model of the Eiffel Tower represents the real thing.

Without imagination, people are not able to relate to the future at all. Imagination is also a source of creativity and trying out new ideas or doing things in new ways. Although it makes use of the knowledge available, an image will always be a product of free creation. By envisaging the future modifies the decisions people make today, which will eventually culminate into the 'yet to come' over time. This balance between knowledge and creativity will be different when dealing with the short-term, the medium-term and the long-term future.

Imagining allows people to render something tangible that is intangible so that people can relate to it (Sartre, 2012). The image is just a means for relating to the object itself. Imagining the future is a way of relating to the future, not to whims.

People can reflect on this by using fictional accounts, for example, using science fiction, to consider 'what if?' In other words, imaginative or creative thinking is the trigger for developing new technologies and social systems, and how images affected the decisions that were made. People also look at the current narratives about imagining people's future, and how that could affect the decisions made today. People discuss the role of knowledge and rationality when people imaginatively make decisions for the future.

With a superior understanding of the relationship between knowledge, imagination and rationality, people will be better equipped for coping with the future. The vagueness of foreseeing the future is ingrained in the unquestionable statement that the future does not (yet) exist. So, the main problem is: how can people relate to a non-extant future?

A conceptual idea is a means of relating to the real thing. In this way, people can imagine situations and careers as well as complex phenomena and relate with them accordingly, although not in identical ways. This process is important for designing scenarios and design thinking discussed in the latter part of this and Chapter 4.

The preceding discussion implies that, since the future does not exist, people's imagination is the principal way of connecting with it. Since the mental images people create are how they consider the future, it is also a means for making decisions. People's decisions are based on knowledge, often supplemented or supplanted by mental images so that what is intended is realised. For example, if a person imagines a career as an astronaut, they will inform themselves about this career by researching facts, data and other information. If they consider becoming an astronaut is a possibility, they imagine themselves in this role or in space, being inside a space ship, conducting space experiments, etc., to facilitate their exploration.

Knowledge and Imagination

Career strategising is based on the creative part of the imaginings people generate. Given intentional visualisation, people will contemplate what underpins their rational reasoning (e.g. emotions, assumptions) which assists in career decision making. On this basis, they feel more confident in planning for their next career step. One of the purposes of visualising the future is to consider the mental image that it is conjured up and to interrogate it (i.e. mull it over) to ascertain whether or not, it is a realistic pursuit given their circumstances and the circumstances of the career itself, for example, will it meet their needs for the future, can they envisage doing the job and/or what sacrifices will they need to make to make it real, and so on.

How is the interaction between knowledge and imagination of the unknown to be rational today, concerning the future and the effect of today's actions in the future? Knowledge and imagination merge in the minds of the decision makers, perhaps unaware that their rationality is built upon that hybrid knowledge. Decisions that have long-term effects are made in an iterative process, where the future is built while adapting to changes in knowledge and imagination, as described by Piaget, assimilating and accommodating them (Chelini & Riva 2013). This iteration process is what creates the possibility of both shaping and coping with the future, where humans imagine and re-imagine situations and technologies according to the knowledge they get and the place where they want to be.

SCENARIO DESIGNING

When crucial factors about careers are not easily quantifiable, it involves the creation of coherent stories about possible future conditions (Alessandri, Ford, Lander, Leggio, & Taylor, 2004). 'A scenario is not a future reality but rather a means to represent it with the aim of clarifying present action in light of possible and desirable futures' (Durance & Godet, 2010, p. 1488).

A scenario is a method for modelling a possible future situation, including prospective outcomes, highlighting key factors that will drive future developments. It is a tool for contextualising the question being investigated. Scenario designing highlights the development of a career strategy that is 'robust' and maintains integrity across different scenarios. Scenario designing is a qualitative tool to aid the decision maker in crafting options relevant to their situation (Dye, 2002).

There are three different types of scenario-methods: prognostic, explorative and normative (Börjeson et al., 2006). For early career participants, the aim is to develop scenarios for promising career pathways. For mid-to-late career participants, the scenario-method is a more analytical one to ascertain what has happened in the past and compare this with future possibilities. This approach could be blended with a normative approach asking 'what should happen' (Börjeson et al., 2006).

A qualification for using explorative scenarios is engaging people, who are well-experienced in career development in a range of industries. One of the main reasons was to encourage as many participants as possible and taking stakeholder's time constraints into account. The central steps are as follows: establishing the scope of the question; collecting and clustering of influencing factors; identifying drivers from the previous list of factors for scenario development; designing the scenario; and, finally, describing the scenario outcome.

Choice making leads eventually to an option that is expected to reap benefits for the individuals concerned. Once the scenarios have been produced, the foremost activity is to formulate a strong strategy that takes into account the majority of conditions characterised in the short list of scenarios (Othman, 2008). Although one of the objectives of scenario designing is to provide a model of uncertainty, it employs relatively simple evaluation techniques to assess and compare the anticipated outcomes of various options (Durbach & Stewart, 2003). Scenario designing and multi-criteria decision analysis are used in conjuction with career strategising (Montibeller, Shaw, & Westcombe, 2006).

In Chapter 2, questions were raised around career thinking and rethinking. Here, it is important to think if not transdisciplinary rather inter-disciplinary. It is time to think of a career as less about the individual experience and more about a cooperative, shared one.

As stated throughout this book, career design is about making choices. Creating career scenarios is about confronting challenges in designing or co-learning a career against a background of uncertainty, change and reality. In the world of work, challenges and opportunities are pursued and eventually matured. Distinctive career capabilities need to be developed and tough strategic choices rare made. Being very creative is one thing, and successfully managing a career portfolio is another. This process necessitates trialling, collaboration, inventiveness change, as well as coping with the contradictory demands between strategic emphasis and elasticity (Bingham, Furr, & Eisenhardt, 2014). It is not merely a question of either/or thinking, rather considering all possibilities, including 'far-out' options (Lewis, Andriopoulos, & Smith, 2014).

As previously noted, scenarios are illustrative narratives of plausible alternative projections of a specific part of the future to shed light on current action, given the possible and desirable futures (Godet, 2001). The purpose of scenario designing is to provide purpose and commitment to designing career for the future (Ratcliffe, 2000; Ringland, 2006) and the result is not an accurate picture of tomorrow (Dye, 2002).

This process is initiated by engaging with others and giving them and you an investment in the outcome. Offsetting intelligent discernment of priorities with a focus on achieving an outcome is important. The process is initiated by advising people what is at stake and getting them to align around the goal of value creation. An orientation towards results is essential. Three processes are important for designing scenarios (Fig. 2):

(a) Ensuring collaboration and commitment to the process. People need to understand the consequences of their engagement on the outcomes.

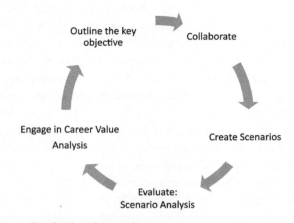

Fig. 2.   Designing Scenarios.

(b)   Underscoring confidence in a person leads to successful
      outcomes even if the engagement process is arduous
      and at times, conflicting. The ability to handle clashing
      viewpoints is invaluable. These meetings are aimed at
      challenging participants and presenting new perspectives.

(c)   Guiding participants through inductive or deductive
      thinking. Inductive thinking requires the group engaging
      in several brainstorming stints, discussing probable
      events in the future, their initiating factors and possible
      consequences. The scenarios are generated based on events
      (Hanafizadeh, Hashemi, & Salahi, 2009). Deductive
      thinking permits the outlining and prioritising of scenarios
      using known factors or drivers (based on Walsh, 2005).

CONCLUSION

Fast forward, there is a difference between short-term and
a long-term perspectives. In the short term, the future is

somehow foreseeable, and current knowledge is useful for understanding the consequences of today's decisions. The challenge arises when making decisions with long-term outcomes. There is less knowledge available about that distant future because it is further removed from the conditions people live in today. Between the present and the distant future, there are developments and changes that people cannot know with any certainty. There is an intrinsic relationship between knowledge and rationality. Knowledge is used to make rational decisions. Now, at this given point in time, there is knowledge available in the form of accumulated facts and scientific developments representing what humanity knows today. Then one can wonder what can replace accumulated knowledge in the process of making rational decisions with long-term effects. People answer that imagination, which of course has a role to play in any form of decision, even in the short term, becomes much more crucially important in dealing with the long-term future. Therefore, people, faced with the lack of knowledge about the future, will imagine it and form choices based on this.

Strategising and developing scenarios or future thinking motivates people to think outside their current boundaries, which is limiting the depth of their information and narrowing their choices. Future-now thinking (Kahn, 1962, p. 60) is central for career thinking as the future remains unknowable and uncertain for those people who are transitioning in their careers and that is most people who are employed in varying capacities, at school or university or contemplating retirement. A different method is used as demonstrated in this chapter as well as the next, which focussed on design thinking. Career thinking is a tricky issue as the decisions made today have lasting consequences not only for the career incumbent but also for those who are financially dependent on them.

REFERENCES

Alessandri, T. M., Ford, D. N., Lander, D. M., Leggio, K. B., & Taylor, M. (2004). Managing risk and uncertainty in complex capital projects. *The Quarterly Review of Economics and Finance*, 44, 751–767.

Barnard, C. (1938). *The functions of the executive*. Cambridge, MA: Harvard University Press.

Bingham, C. B., Furr, N. R., & Eisenhardt, K. M. (2014). The opportunity paradox. *MIT Sloan Management Review*, 56(1), 29–35.

Börjeson, L., Hojer, M., Dreborg, k-H., Ekvall, T., & Finnvedin, G. (2006). Scenario types and techniques. Towards a user's guide. *Futures*, 38, 723–739. doi:10.1016/j.futures.2005.12.002

Chelini, C., & Riva, S. (2013). On the relationships between Friedrich Hayek and Jean Piaget: A new paradigm for cognitive and evolutionary economists. In R. Frantz, & R. Leeson (Eds.), *Hayek and behavioural economics. Archival insights into the evolution of economics series* pp. 127–148. London: Palgrave Macmillan.

Chiappe, D., Kennedy, J. M. & Smykowski, T. (2003). Reversibility, aptness, and the conventionality of metaphors and similes. *Metaphor Symb.*, 18, 85–105.

Cruz, Di., & Meisenbach, R. (2018). Expanding role boundary management theory: How volunteering highlights contextually shifting strategies and collapsing work–life role boundaries. *Human Relations*, 71(2), 182–205.

Durance, P., & Godet, M. (2010). Scenario building: Uses and abuses. *Technological Forecasting and Social Change*, 77(9), 1488–1492.

Durbach, L., & Stewart, J. (2003). Integrating scenario planning and goal programming. *Journal of Multi-Criteria Decision Analysis*, 12, 261–271.

Dweck, C. S. (1996). Implicit theories as organisers of goals and behaviour. In P. M. Gollwitzer & J. A. Bargh (Eds.), *The psychology of action. Linking cognition and motivation to behaviour* (pp. 69–90). New York, NY: Guildford Press.

Dye, L. D. (2002). Using scenario planning as an aid in project portfolio management. In *Proceedings of the Project Management Institute Annual Seminars and Symposium*, October 3–10, San Antonio, TX.

Dyer, J., Gregersen, H., & Christensen, C. M. (2011). *The innovator's DNA*. Boston, MA: Harvard Business Review Press.

Epstein, S. (1994). Integration of the cognitive and the psychodynamic unconscious. *American Psychologist*, 49(8), 709–724.

Ferrari, L., Sgaramella, M. T., & Soresi, S. (2015). Bridging disability and work – Contribution and challenges of life design. In L. Nota & J. Rossier (Eds.), *Handbook of life design* (pp. 219–232). Göttingen, Germany: Hogrefe.

Gentner, D., & Gentner, D. R. (1983). Flowing waters and teeming crowds: Mental models of electricity. In D. Gentner & A. L. Stevens (Eds.), *Mental models hillsdale* (pp. 99–129). Hillsdale, NJ: Erlbaum.

Gerrig, R. J., & Gibbs, R. W., Jr. (1988). Beyond the lexicon: Creativity in language production. *Metaphor and Symbolic Activity*, *3*, 1–19.

Godet, M. (2001). *Creating futures: Scenario planning as a strategic management tool*. London: Economical Publishing.

Hanafizadeh, P., Hashemi, A., & Salahi, P. E. (2009). Robust strategic planning employing scenario planning and fuzzy inference system. *International Journal of Decision Support Systems Technology*, *1*(3), 21–45.

Hurson, T. (2008). *Think better*. New York, NY: McGraw-Hill.

Kahn, H. (1962). *Thinking About the Unthinkabl*. New York: Horizon.

Kendall-Taylor, N., & Haydon, A. (2014a). Using metaphor to translate the science of resilience and developmental outcomes. *Public Underst. Sci.*, *25*, 576–587.

Kendall-Taylor, N., & Haydon, A. (2014b). Space to think: Using metaphor to expand public thinking about criminal justice reform. *Stud. Media Commun.*, *2*, 13–23.

Kounios, J., & Beeman, M. (2014). The cognitive neuroscience of insight. *Annual Review of Psychology*, *65*, 71–93.

Lewis, M. W., Andriopoulos, C., & Smith, W. K. (2014). Paradoxical leadership to enable strategic agility. *California Management Review*, *56*(3), 58–77.

Lindblom, C. (2010). The science of 'muddling' through. *Emergence: Complexity and Organisation*, *12*(1), 70–80.

Lindblom, C. E. (1979). Still muddling, not yet through. *Public Administration Review*, *39*, 517–526.

Masdonati, J., & Fournier, G. (2015). Life design, young adults, and the school-to-work transition. In L. Nota & J. Rossier (Eds.), *Handbook of life design* (pp. 117–134). Göttingen, Germany: Hogrefe.

Mattimore, B. W. (2012). *Idea stormers*. San Francisco, CA: Jossey-Bass.

Montibeller, G., Shaw, D., & Westcombe, M. (2006). Using decision support systems to facilitate the social process of knowledge management. *Knowledge Management Research & Practice*, 4(2), 125–137.

Moser, K. S., Clases, C., & Wehner, T. (2000). Taking actors' perspectives seriously: Whose knowledge and what is managed? Knowledge management in a transdisciplinary perspective. In R. Häberli, R. W. Scholz, A. Bill, & M. Welti (Eds.), *Transdisciplinarity: Joint problem-solving among science, technology and society* (Vol. I, pp. 534–538). Zurich, Switzerland: Haffmans Sachbuch Verlag.

Nota, L., Ginevra, M. C., & Santilli, S. (2015). Life design and prevention. In L. Nota & J. Rossier (Eds.), *Handbook of life design* (pp. 183–199). Göttingen, Germany: Hogrefe.

Nyhan, B., & Reifler, J. (2010). When corrections fail: The persistence of political misperceptions. *Polit. Behav.*, 32, 303–330.

Onora, N (1975). *Acting on principle: An essay in Kantian ethics*. New York, NY: Columbia University Press.

Othman, R. (2008). Enhancing the effectiveness of the balanced scorecard with scenario planning. *International Journal of Productivity and Performance Management*, 57(3), 259–266.

Ottati, V., Rhoads, S., & Graesser, A. C. (1999). The effect of metaphor on processing style in a persuasion task: A motivational resonance model. *Journal of Personality and Social Psychology*, 77(4), 688–697.

Piaget, J. (1955). Perceptual and cognitive (or operational). Structures in the development of the concept of space in the child. *Acta Psychologica*, 11, 41–46.

Ratcliffe, J. (2000). Scenario building: A suitable method for strategic property planning. *Property Management*, 18(2), 127–144.

Ringland, G. (2006). *Scenario planning: Managing for the future* (2nd ed.). Oxford: John Wiley and Sons.

Sartre, J.-P. (2012). *The imagination*. London: Routledge.

Savickas, M. L. (2015). Life design with adults – Developmental individualization using biographical bricolage. In L. Nota & J. Rossier (Eds.), *Handbook of life design* (pp. 135–150). Göttingen, Germany: Hogrefe.

Sawer, M. (2012). Gender and institutions: Room with a view? *Australian Feminist Studies*. 27(73), 325–330.

Simon, H. A., & Newell, A. (1958). Heuristic problem solving: The next advance in operations research. *Operations Research*, 6(1), 1–10.

Solomon, R. C. (1993). *The passions: Emotions and the meaning of life*. Indianapolis, IN: Hackett.

Sternberg, R. J. (2014). The development of adaptive competence. *Developmental Review*, 34, 208–224.

Thibodeau, P. & Boroditsky, L. (2011). Metaphors we think with: The role of metaphor in reasoning. PLoS ONE, 6, e16782.

Vosniadou, S., & Ortony, A. (Eds.). (1989). *Similarity and analogical reasoning*. New York, NY: Cambridge University Press.

Walsh, P. R. (2005). Dealing with the uncertainties of environmental change by adding scenario planning to the strategy reformulation equation. *Management Decision, 43*(1), 113–122.

Weber, M., Baehr, P. R., & Wells, G. R. (2002). *The Protestant ethic and the spirit of capitalism and other writings*. London: Penguin 20th Centrury Classics.

Weick, K. (2002). Puzzles in organisational learning: An exercise in disciplined imagination. *British Journal of Management, 13*, S7–S15.

Weller, A., Villejoubert, G., & Vallée-Tourangeau, F. (2011). Interactive insight problem solving. *Thinking and Reasoning, 17*, 424–439.

4

DESIGN THINKING A CAREER

INTRODUCTION

Design thinking has its roots in the mid-twentieth century (Simon, 1969) and is employed today to engage the new or repurposing of an idea for a different outcome. It is applicable for career development, particularly as people transition through career stages and considers either trying something new or re-inventing themselves. Design thinking is a people-centric approach for deliberating about innovation and invention aimed at targeting peoples' needs and preferences so that they are integrated into the outcome. Through the generation of new ideas, people gain new insights and balance diverse perspectives into a whole, that is, integrative thinking. Integrative thinking is

> *the ability to face constructively the tension of*
> *opposing models and instead of choosing one at*
> *the expense of the other, to generate a creative*
> *resolution of the tension in the form of a new*
> *model that contains elements of the individual*
> *models but is superior to each (Martin, 2007, p. 7).*

An overview of the design thinking literature shows that there are many representations of design thinking with no definitive list of characteristics (Hassi & Laakso, 2011). What is definitive is that it is people-centred, driven by collaboration and ability to be tested in practice through prototyping.

Career development and entrepreneurship are similar. Unique and significant challenges in creating careers are stimulating and resource intensive, as is the pathway for any entrepreneur and an innovator. In a similar way to entrepreneurship, searching and forging career pathways is complex due to balancing and offsetting the needs and costs of multiple stakeholders.

Given the age of disruption, careers increasingly require a creative approach to finding solutions to so-called 'wicked problems' (Koh, Chai, Wong, & Huang-Yao, 2015). This approach is also comparable to the ways and means used by entrepreneurs. Career mentors and coaches can guide people since they have deep industry experience. Increasingly, people need to investigate innovative or alternative approaches to a career as well as to seek out support and resources. This process adds to the complexity of career development due to higher personal investment and greater ambiguity (Lenton et al., 2014).

The purpose of design thinking is to investigate 'messy' problems (e.g. Brown, 2008; Glen, Suciu, & Baughn, 2014). Career thinking is one of those 'messy' problems, entailing human decision-making about time, effort and money. Design thinking helps to take into account the bases upon which choices are made, defending choices and translating these into career choice sets.

This chapter outlines a framework to guide people through career innovation and development to address their personalised needs and demands. The reason for using this approach is that career experience is a relative experience and thereby lacking a universal prescription. Design thinking also shows the significance of the incremental discovery, collaboration and thinking about the issue from multiple perspectives (e.g. colleagues, peoples, clients and customers; Brown, 2008). The process further demonstrates the power of narrative-making as a design thinking tool.

CAREER DESIGNERS

Designing careers is a strategy of modifying existing careers, focussing on technological innovations to ascertain new careers or centred on new services that people will need in the future. It is important to understand the underlying processes by asking: what are we designing, why are we designing this career or set of careers in this way, and how are we designing them.

A career designer is anyone who has an interest in developing a career for themselves or someone else; they are skilled navigators (Badke, 2012). The career designer needs to realise what they value in potential careers, including strengths in terms of skills, knowledge and attributes and whom they know (their network of contacts). An overriding aspiration is essential for this process (Sarasvathy, 2001). The challenge for people, concerned about their next career step even if it is their initial one, is how to transform intangible aspirations into tangible outcomes that they perceive to be valuable.

A conventional career planning approach by career specialists is based on individual demographic and ideological characteristics. This approach rests on individual knowledge, attitudes and also assumes that a person's career engagement is primarily an individual choice and not greatly affected by social and cultural systems and values.

DESIGN THINKING FOR CAREER DEVELOPMENT

Design thinking is an innovative approach to career change and is influenced by subjective, emotional and, sometimes, multi-generational attachments to 'career' shaping – identities, dependence on careers for meaning, satisfaction and fulfilment. Yet, at the same time, career attachment is conceptualised and enacted in a way that often disengages a person from their career, for example, if someone fears or denies the need for a career change and does not act on this perceiving that they will be worse off if they do so (Table 1).

An important model for educational institutions is to partner with adult learners to facilitate their participation in curriculum design. In today's digitally connected, globalised

Table 1. Conventional Career Planning with a Design Thinking Approach.

Criteria	Conventional Career Planning	Design Thinking
Underlying assumptions	Rationality, objectivity, evidence and quantifiable	Immersive experience in career journey
Method	The predefined pathway from education origin, for example, school or university	Experimentation – iterating towards the optimal solution
Process	Planning	'What-if?' scenario
Decision Drivers	Educate, employment foothold and promotion	Empathic insight; experiential career modelling
Values	Secure, stability and certainty	Enthusiasm, creativity and personal fulfilment
Level of focus	Employers and management	Individual

world, didactic pedagogy is at variance with expectations of both students and employers. The learning journey is formed by the need to bridge the gap between knowledge creation and action in transforming concepts to feasible realities. A design learning approach is a way to step back and determine what the problem was in terms of dissatisfaction with the current approach to shape an empathetic, human-centric lens on what could be. Fig. 1 shows this approach.

Human-centric Learning

Design thinking is a human-centric process of learning that focuses on 'making' solutions (Kelley & Kelley, 2013). This process develops implicitly and intuitively drawing upon experience, with people participating in practice (Schön, 1984). Using this approach, educational institutions engage prospective adult learners, employers and others within a collaborative, design process. This approach also overcomes the

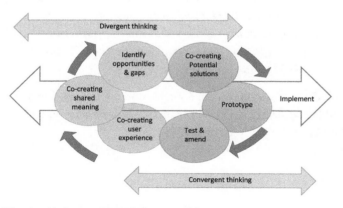

Fig. 1.   Human-centred Co-creation.

Source: Based on Burkhardt (2009).

'problem of practice' (City, Elmore, Fiarman, & Teitel, 2009), convoluted conundrums with no simple solution.

Applying Design Thinking to Learning: Definition and Principles

The principles and methodology of *Design Thinking* (see Rowe, 1991; Simon, 1967) potentially guide and assist learners in assuming responsibility, shape and navigate their human journey no matter the destiny. Design thinking links learning principles (Ramsden, 1992) with more intuitive thinking to meet the needs of learners that are technically feasible and viable for achieving sustainable outcomes. By applying design learning as a learning framework, it is considered '..... both a mechanism for learning .... [simultaneously] a learning process' (Dym, Agogino, Eris, Frey, & Leifer, 2005, p. 112). The methodical fusion of skills, knowledge and practices of design learning exemplify

> ... *a systematic approach with rules based on evidence and a set of contextualized practices that are constantly adapting to circumstances. It is a skillful, creative activity that can be improved on with reflection and scholarship (Beetham & Sharpe, 2007, p. 6).*

Courses would be then designed and implemented in a feasible and strategic way and evaluated by how they function in practice (Kelley & Littman, 2001).

Design Learning in Practice

Action and experiential learning are not novel pedagogical methods. What is new is inviting students to play an active role.

They enter a more collaborative relationship with curriculum designers, facilitating both a generation of knowledge and understanding '…. that lead to the acquisition of both disciplinary knowledge, personal and interpersonal skills; and product, process and system building skills' (Crawley et al., 2014, p. 29).

Design learning is a practice that integrates a sequence of connected and iterative steps, used to approach, reframe and solve ill-defined, 'real world' problems, across a varied collection of situations. Participants contribute and form knowledge, thus developing emotional intelligence by trial and error method using their senses and actions to facilitate the outcomes. It is genuine, engaged learning and transformation.

This process progressed to developing a suitable 'preliminary prototype' for shaping learning and teaching strategy. Designing a curriculum with adult learners necessitates a democratic, active and stratified instruction that facilitates learning. Choices are unpacked to ascertain underlying assumptions, values and beliefs that are critical for all designers engaged in the process. Further, it is about working collaboratively to enhance the lives and well-being of learners and, in doing so, to draw from as many different perspectives as possible that bear on the complex matters of today (Vianna, Vianna, Adler, Lucena, & Russo, 2012).

The outcome of this approach is that courses designed and delivered are a closer fit to the needs of what students are grappling with – up-skilled strategies for their working and professional lives. At the same time, this approach would employ students' real-life experiences to rejuvenate and align learning to potential career paths and life journeys. An approach such as this would help educational institutions encourage academics to think like designers to retreat from passive teaching approaches, and to focus on active, experiential and problem-based learning (Glen, Suciu, Baughn, & Anson, 2015).

Design thinking is a symbiotic process for people to explore their career journey – past, present and future – through a series of prisms. There are several principles to guide a person through designing a career. The process engages both simultaneously divergent and convergent thinking, as outlined below:

(a) Inquiry-based;

(b) Personally directed;

(c) Collaboratively driven; and

(d) Action-orientated outcomes.

New Career Horizons

Design thinking opens up new and diverse career horizons for people to consider through a defined process commencing with the current situation, reflecting on the past and moving them to a future position. The process maintains a momentum energising their thinking, propelling their thoughts towards the future. Along the way, the person engages in a guided discovery of their capability, career options and aligning one to the other in a deeply reflective process. The outcome of the process is to design a career prototype for participants to implement and monitor their performance, should they decide to embark on this career pathway. Design thinking is applicable for candidates from novice through to highly experienced, as shown in Fig. 2.

While design thinking is applicable in numerous contexts, the focus of this chapter is applying its principles to the career development process (including invention, implementation and evaluation of careers and employability programmes). The process of design thinking is beneficial as a skill for anyone considering prospects whether these are school students

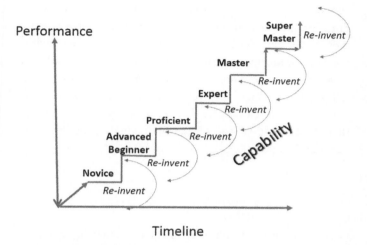

Timeline

Fig. 2.   A Capability Pathway.

or someone transitioning to active requirement learning. A people-centred, collaborative and well-rounded approach enables greater receptiveness to people's needs, maximises mutual benefit through co-creation of value and boosts the probability of effective engagement.

People-centred Career Design

The people-centred element is one of the defining elements of the design thinking philosophy: involving people in the design and career development process that meets their needs and preferences (Brown, 2008; Glen et al., 2014; Hassi & Laakso, 2011).

The complexity of careers requires both career-designing and career-doing skills; both sets important for either designing or working in a career. From a career design perspective, the first set of skills involves direct control over the trajectory of the career journey and the latter set entails skills that enhance the person's capability to drive their career in the direction they wish to take it while simultaneously enriching their career experience. Both sets of skills promote activities relevant for an employee working in government or industry.

Participants collaborating in design thinking for careers will need to interact effectively in the group, receive and provide useful and relevant feedback, and focus on career design that is personalised for specific individuals including their needs and values.

Collaborative Career Design

Collaboration is a symbiosis, an equal partnership comprising diverse stakeholders, integral to design thinking. It is a cooperative approach, ideal for solving complex problems leading to the incorporation of several perspectives and knowledge sources (e.g. quantitative, qualitative, technical and opinion) (Hassi & Laakso, 2011) as well as stimulating innovation (Benson & Dresdow, 2014). At the core of collaboration, if appropriately facilitated, people observe and understand each other's needs and preferences that learn to create value through potential partnerships with employers, for example (Amit & Zott, 2002). In that sense, collaboration is a meaningful social practice. Embracing a well-rounded interpretation is a distinctive feature of design thinking, and involves understanding of not only utilitarian demands but also social, emotional and cultural demands, all of which are context and interest-specific (Hassi & Laakso, 2011). This equation is judicious for understanding the career landscape within which innovations are being developed.

Collaboration is also ideal for integrative thinking. In an age of specialisation, which characterises much of the latter half of the twentieth century, most people are not skilled in thinking across disciplinary boundaries. Collaboration affords participants the opportunity to canvass ideas that are different and even clash with their own. Strategising and design thinking creates a situation where participants confront different and novel ideas and navigate through the inconsistencies, at times, embracing them.

The process requires some degree of shared decision-making, reciprocal respect and trust among the group. The group needs to balance the integration of the career design strategy (e.g. information and knowledge transfer among participants) while co-ordinating the logistics of the collaborative process (e.g. collective learning and communication).

Design Thinking Career – Process

Exercise: What Is 'Your Story'?

Participants write a brief narrative about their career story to initiate the process: past, present and future. Initially, it is a stream of consciousness writing, mimicking a real-life and internal dialogue. This written piece is deeply personal, read only by the author. There should be no concern for writing style punctuation, grammar, etc. In other words, participants are pretty much letting their thoughts flood onto the page without imposing any structure on them.

To assist writing 'your story', consider addressing the following list of questions.

(a) Who are you, and what outcome do you wish to accomplish?

(b) What work would you like to do? Why are you interested in this type of work?

(c) What are your values?

(d) Why does this work fit with those values?

(e) What skills would like to develop? Why?

(f) What skills do you have now?

(g) What do people say you are good at?

(h) What do you imagine to realise from this work in the
     long run? Why is this important to you?

(i) How will this work benefit you? Others? Your family?

Story writing for career planning has a number of advantages for participants, drawing them deeply into their thoughts.

Interrogate the written narrative as follows:

(1) Does it have a point of view?

(2) Is there one story or many?

(3) Dissect it to identify and isolate distinctive story points.

(4) Prioritise your story points, and colour code them.

Develop a career statement
For example, I want to become a corporate lawyer as it provides the opportunity to

(a) Assist others.

(b) Be challenged intellectually.

(c) Diverse practice areas.

(d) Work in a good organisation environment.

(e) Learn transferable skills.

(f) Work internationally.

Prepare to implement your career plans
When? Work out what you can do

(1) immediately;

(2) in less than 6 months;

(3) within 6–12 months; and

(4) in greater than 12 months, for example, gaining a credential.

Create Milestones in Career Plan

(a) Organise so that all the shortest actions are completed ASAP

(b) Organise the requirements for completing the longer-term tasks

(c) Gain an internship

(d) Join a professional association for networking experience

Example of a Career Statement

I propose to work for five years at a challenging, cutting edge legal firm to bolster my skill development, professional networks and expand my knowledge of legal cases.

After 5 years:

I will apply for a legal role in another country where the legal system is similar to mine.

Exercise for the Career Specialist

Analyse a current point in time working with one or more people focussing on a career transition. Who are they? What do they want? Several other questions emerge such as categories given in Fig. 3a. Use these as a guide for developing further questions.

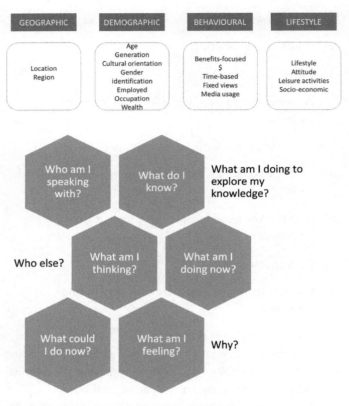

Fig. 3a and b.   Structuring Career Guidance.

Fig. 3b guides the career incumbent through the following questions focussing on core issues as follows:

(a) What does a person perceive? How does their environment appear to them? What offers have they had so far? What is working well for them? What is not? Why? Who are their family, friends and partners?

(b) What is a person attending to? What are they learning from friends, candidates, supervisor and colleagues or social media?

(c) What is a person thinking? What is important to them? What are their dreams?

(d) What is a person feeling? What concerns them now? What will concern them in the future? What are they currently doing? What are their typical activities now? Whom are they interacting with? Which networks are they using: person to person, social media or both?

(e) What are the person's pain points? What are the most frustrating things about career exploring or journeying for them? What challenges and risks are they facing every day?

(f) What are the person's advantages? What makes them content? What are their career preferences, all things being equal? What does career success look like? How are they fulfilling their career goals now? If not, why not?

PHASES OF THE CAREER DESIGN PROCESS

It is helpful to clarify what the genuine interest is, to prevent leaping ahead to try to achieve a career solution or outcome. This process involves distinguishing between actionable interests and circumstances that cannot be immediately solved. Tables 2 and 3 show these phases in two levels: macro and micro perspectives.

Brainstorming

When people face a career challenge, they are often at a loss in knowing where to start. People need to learn how to generate

Table 2. Phases of the Career Design Process – Macro.

Exploration	Creation	Reflection	Implementation
Understand the person's needs, motivations, expectations, career provider's processes and constraints	Develop solutions to address the person's interests	Test potential solutions with candidates and experts	Define processes and deliverables
Identify interests from a person's perspective	Engage in the trial-and-error creation process with the potential person	Provide career stories to convey the concept	Train employees on processes
		Integrate feedback and improve concepts	Set up processes and structures in career contexts

Table 3. Phases of the Career Design Process – Micro.

Phases	Aims	Methods
Exploration	Learn about candidates' needs, motivations and behavioural patterns	Interviews
	Explore career options	Interviews
	Develop a tangible, intuitive picture of potential career personas	Personas
	Understand the costs and requirements associated with each career	Is the person seeking professional career support?
Creation	Develop ideas for career concepts	Brainstorming
	Communicate concepts	Paper prototyping
	Review career options	Redesign career options

Reflection	Test early concepts with potential candidates	Storytelling
	Communicate concepts using stories	Seek their feedback
Implement	New proposed career option	Changes to accommodate capability and specific circumstances

ideas and imagine outcomes to ascertain how might a career is created. Generating ideas is important as it gets them to converge on the challenge. Initiate the process by asking three questions:

(a) What is the context I would like to work in? Contexts differ greatly, and so do the answers appropriate to those contexts. List them in Column A.

(b) What is the demand for skills in the context? List them in Column B.

(c) Commence brainstorming options using these parameters and use each idea to trigger the next one.

It is not always about coming up with the most innovative idea for designing a career, rather the most suitable one. A tool that is useful for individuals and groups is one based on brainstorming principles. Brainstorming is an effective skill to stimulate thinking (Bittner, Bruena, & Rietzschel, 2016; Curşeu & Brink, 2016; Korde & Paulus, 2017; Lebuda, Galewska-Kustra, & Glăveanu, 2016). Brainstorming facilitates splitting the challenge into components. How could the puzzle be viewed in a new way so that each part could be seen separately from the whole? Understanding the parts helps to make sense of the whole.

The originator of brainstorming, Osborn (1963) outlined four principles to guide brainstorming: first, the deferment of judgment to extend the range of ideas or options; second, quantifying sets of suggestions; third, engaging in free-wheeling thinking; and, finally, integrating options to narrow the range of ideas. Inhibiting evaluation diminishes people's concerns about 'being wrong', or alternatively, defending their view and widens the possibility of thinking creatively. If so, brainstorming is highly engaging and not in the least, de-motivating (De Dreu, Baas, & Nijstad, 2008). Consequently, by withholding the tendency to evaluate and critique, people are open to generating different options, maximising their options and willing to question their generic beliefs or stereotypes.

Self-evaluation is a process of formulating positive or negative feedback (Hattie & Timperley, 2007) and impedes creative thinking. For example, positive feedback, especially when others (e.g. a career counsellor) provide it, steers individuals into a particular direction. Therefore, it has a similar outcome as negative feedback in shutting down their options. Design thinking allows people the freedom to explore 'left-field' ideas which they can use these to investigate some career pathways.

Smart Choices

At the next stage, ask 'which pathway will work for me?' to explore further even if feeling apprehensive at this stage. If there are more then two pathways, join them together to narrow the choice by asking questions as follows:

(a) Skill and knowledge requirements?

(b) Additional learning?

(c) Existing capabilities?

(d) Career culture, for example, teaching, scientist and policy analyst?

(e) Workplace culture, for example, school, university and a government agency?

(f) Workload demands, for example, paperwork, publishing pressure and working hours?

(g) Career benefits, for example, vacations and working with politicians?

(h) Work and family considerations, for example, flexible working options?

Given the above considerations, then ask 'under what conditions would I favour one pathway over another?'

Career thinking and addressing challenges are not easy. It is important that people consider situations in which they can maximise their attributes and capability to consider career options. This is not straightforward due to perceived limitations leading to feeling 'stuck' or what Dweck (1996) and Goleman (2006) refer to as a fixed mindset, that is, believing that it is impossible change or there is no room for growth. It is important that individuals are encouraged to think perceptively if they are to maximise their potential. Learning is the key for a flexible mindset.

CAREER MINDSET

Developing a suitable mindset, that is, a perspective based on growth, is significant in achieving outcomes (Yeager et al., 2016). A negative or fixed mindset is a deterrent; once a person is in it, it blinds them for seeing other things, making them less flexible to take on new ideas, especially blocking new information; linking ideas or thinking 'what if?' A negative mindset essentially blocks interrogation, a vital strategy for problem-solving and creative thinking. Having slipped into a rigid mindset, people cease to examine and often fail to identify the most evident aspects of their conundrum.

Design thinking relies on the capacity and confidence to engage in diverse mindsets depending on the dictates of the situation. Table 4 shows four diverse, inter-related mindsets, and the respective qualities of each.

Mindsets are shaped by people's experiences, learned knowledge, values, interactions with others, a risk appetite as well as a person's predispositions. All these features are subject to change overtime. Mindsets 'grow' overtime. Flexible thinking requires a diversity of mindset and open to the flow of ideas from various sources; otherwise, they become bound by their own thinking, that is, a fixed mindset.

Table 4. Qualities of Mindsets.

Nature of Mindset	Qualities
Universal	Thinking beyond a person's current boundaries, for example, metropolitan and national
	Valuing integration
	Welcoming cultural diversity
Courageous pioneering	Thinking beyond current knowledge boundaries
	Valuing knowledge and skill integration
	Valuing continuous development and enhancement
	Tapping into diverse sources of knowledge
	Taking deliberate risks
Practical	Focus on cost-effectiveness
	Analysing core skills
	Developing skills and knowledge
Co-operative	Realising spatial, temporal, and cultural opportunities
	Valuing complementarity
	Sharing talent and know-how
	Negotiating boundaries and limits

Nudging Flexible Thinking

When a person's mindset is fixed, they come to a standstill. It is difficult to nudge them from this standpoint. A nudge is about facilitating a rapid learning feedback loop to facilitate 'unfreezing' of the mind while remaining mindful of how people learn. The career incumbent needs to be at the centre of the 'career exploration process' not the career guide. Rather, anyone facilitating this process needs to support an iterative and integrative thinking approach while providing a relevant career-thinking framework. With these factors in mind, inductive reasoning is a useful and relevant tool for nudging people's thinking. This process of inductive reasoning guides the person's thinking process. Inductive reasoning works by moving from specific observations made by the career person in the situation to broader generalisations and explanations expressed to the guide. It is a 'grounded' approach leading people to formulate tentative suggestions that are explored with the career incumbent. This process leads to new learning, 'a take away', to consider further or apply.

Guided Reflection

The reflection process is similar to single- versus double-loop learning. It facilitates deep learning and uncovering a situation's potential impacts and influences a person's underlying actions and subsequent impacts.

Double-loop learning assists a person in seeing and dissecting second- and third-order concerns other than the obvious first-order ones (see Argyris & Schön, 1996). According to Ayrgris (2000), learning occurs when inconsistencies or misjudgements are noticed, and an attempt is made to ameliorate these. In double-loop learning, people gain diverse understandings, both surface and deep, which enables them to defend their decision (Argyris & Schön, 1996).

Single-loop learning does not uncover underlying assumptions that are tacit and rarely challenged or if so, readily dismissed. It avoids what is decisive and pervasive in the situation when there is a career choice or an outcome that people resist. Instead of reverting and questioning what led to the outcome, people tend to suppress what one is thinking/feeling and rationality prevails (e.g. the facts are given and the same for all concerned). The results for the participants are what Argyris (1985) refers to as a skilled lack of awareness and skilled incompetence. As the career person brings skilled unawareness into the conversation, the guide needs to understand the possibility of this as well as being amenable to dealing with it. For example, if a person's application for a job is unsuccessful, they will typically explain away their failure as not being suitable for the role, poor capability match or performing poorly at the interview. People rarely question their underlying assumptions unless prompted to do so. Single-loop learning requires robust insights into situations and necessitates a double-loop learning process to overcome this type of surface learning. Double-loop learning will be explored in detail below.

In design thinking a career, there is more than one 'right' outcome. The dilemma is to decide which one is the best. In many ways, it emulates the career conundrum in a non-design thinking setting, when a person has more than one viable career options. In both situations, the dilemma leads to feelings of distress. One way out of this is for the career guide to lead the career person through a guided reflection to double-loop learning, as depicted in Fig. 4.

An example of a set of questions for a guided reflection is as follows:

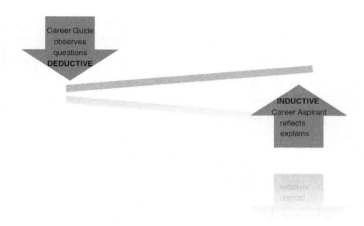

Fig. 4.   Guided Reflection.

(1) Understand your feelings and label them. Query the reason for this feeling.

(2) Explore each option in detail.

(3) Engage your imagination – picture yourself in the career, what would it look like on a daily basis, for example? It is important to understand the positive and negative issues as well as what you would regret in taking one option over the other.

(4) Thoroughly evaluate each option using the information gleaned from the above three stages. For example,

    (a) Which stakeholders impacted by this option, and how? In other words, what are the foreseeable outcomes of my decision? For example, will I need to relocate, and how will this affect my partner and my family? Will my parents support me in this choice? How will my current employer view it?

(b) What duties or responsibilities do I owe these stakeholders? Do I owe a special duty to my current employer?

(c) Does this option efficiently allocate benefits and burdens?

(d) Would I prefer this choice if I was the one adversely impacted by it? For example, if my partner took this option, and I had to deal with the consequences.

(e) How would I feel if everyone selected this option in a similar situation? Is this option in harmony with my values and interests?

(f) What type of professional might I become if I choose this option and ones similar to it on a continuing basis? What does this option say about me?

Action-orientated Learning

Learning is an information processing activity of knowledge creation and sharing that ultimately changes or modifies the action. The capacity to understand performance from cognition leads to the forging of individual and shared/team ideas methods for doing things that directly influences performance (Cooke et al., 2001).

In the explanation of this learning process in organisations, researchers refer to different stages and processes like acquisition, dissemination, interpretation and implementation, all of which imply bringing about new relationships and explanations of phenomena (Brattesta, 2011).

Action-orientated learning is a knowledge shared between individuals, groups and across the organisation that is either invented, tested or re-invented (Dicle & Kose, 2014).

There are disruptions in organisational learning, which are culturally embedded and often impede learning through one or more of the following:

(a) Role-constrained learning: Effective learning and action are prevented due to role constraints or standard operating procedures.

(b) Individual action and organisational action are often misaligned.

(c) Illogical learning and faulty inferences characterise the learning, as there are many missing links in the individual and organisational action where the role of career is unclear.

(d) Learning under ambiguity: Ambiguous and unclear causal connections among the variables, as there is no conceptual learning.

(e) Situational learning: Learning is situation-bound, and there is no generalisation across similar situations.

(f) Individual learning is not shared with relevant others.

(g) Opportunistic learning: The organisation indulges in unpredictable ways of doing things (based on March & Oslen, 1975).

Similarly, March (1991) differentiates between two different types of learning – exploitative and explorative. The difference in terminology is instructive. The former is a process of learning brought about in the context of what is currently known. The latter is a process of learning focussed on learning new information and embracing a diverse path to goal accomplishment which is considered similar to either multiplicative, second-order learning, groundbreaking or action-orientated (Roome & Wijen, 2006).

Double-loop Learning

As indicated above, double-loop learning is a meta-cognitive process that necessitates people retracing their thinking to reflect on the reasoning that led their actions; discovering the thinking that resulted in a specific outcome. See Fig. 5. It is important to employ 'why' questioning, following 'what led to this outcome?' Why? The why is composed of the particular thinking and reasoning related to this situation and these specific actions.

Eventually, a person understands an assessment of the situation based on the Single-Loop Learning Model 1 (referred to in Chapter 2), whereas the Double-Loop Learning Model II allows a person to reflect on what is or might be happening. It is difficult for people to think in a double-loop way. The reason for this is most people's assumptions about why things happen the way they do are reinforced continuously over many decades. It will take time for people to appreciate the Double-Loop Learning Model II unless they have been previously exposed to that way of not only thinking but also acting. It takes skill and confidence not only to see this but also to act upon it. People are less inclined to modify their thinking and best not be forced to do so. There are no guarantees about this and reflection is not rushed to get to a resolution.

Double-loop learning occurs when miscalculations are modified by changing the overarching assumptions in Box A in Fig. 5, followed by the actions as outlined in Box B or C.

This iterative method facilitates learning over time. Through double-loop learning, people progressively supplant their assumptions about careers and themselves. This conversion is a response to a stimulus when confronting a challenge coupled with uncertainty. Conventional or existing assumptions provide little utility for addressing these challenges and require insightful reflection and perspective transformations, which is the beauty of double-loop learning.

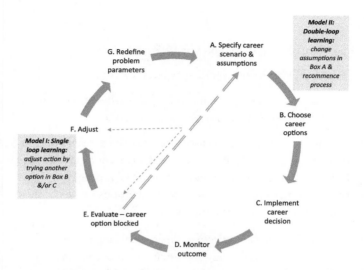

Fig. 5.   Single-loop and Double-loop Learning Framework.

MAPPING A CAREER JOURNEY FOR A PERSON

Phase 1

(a) What is the most recent experience of employment?
      What is full-time, part-time, casual, internship or other?

(b) What was the nature of the work? Think about the
      context of the work, its tasks, purpose and methodology.

(c) What was the outcome? Was it meaningful?
      Memorable? Why? Why not?

(d) What are the various roles that you have had in the
      past? Which ones were meaningful? Memorable? Why?
      Why not?

(e) What difficulties did you encounter?

(f) Did you overcome these or not?

Phase 2

(a) Draft a story based on your answers in Phase 1.

(b) Highlight the outstanding aspects for you.

(c) Canvass some optional career goals with them – choose the main one first and explore this further.

Career strategising consists of generating possible options or scenarios for a future career and then crafting strategies based upon these scenario parameters. It is important to focus on exploring the opposite of their expectations as well as their expectations through the following:

(1) *Outline the key objective.* The crucial starting point for scenario designing for careers is to outline the key objectives for the participant(s) (Dye, 2002). The time horizon and various context(s) for the scenario process are ascertained at this stage.

(2) *Select participants.* Participants can number 1–4, preferably in any one group. Career strategising is conducted with multiple groups simultaneously, perhaps into different groups. Some groups focussing on 'what is'; others focussing on 'what if?' and others playing devil's advocate focussing on 'why not..?'.

(3) *Collaborate.* The collaboration focuses on producing detailed, realistic scenarios involving qualitative consensus building through trial and error interactions. This process produces multiple perceptions and screens as possible, using groups taking a different focus, as suggested above in (2). Idea generation is achieved using various methods (including databases, brainstorming, search conferences, crowdsourcing and open-innovation) (Hirst, Van Knippenberg, Chen, & Sacramento, 2011).

(4) *Identify key decision factors/ driving forces*. In this step, factors that will positively or negatively influence the scenario outcomes are identified. Using the *ESTOPPEL* approach, Table 5, adapted from Linstone (1984), employs the perspectives as both driving forces and inhibitors of change. No value judgments are made at this point.

(5) *Identify complexities, uncertainties*. The next step is the ranking of the key decision factors and the driving forces based on two criteria (Dye, 2002; Ratcliffe, 2000); specifically, the gradation of significance for the success of the issue designated in step one; and the extent of uncertainty surrounding these variables. Work out three or four factors or trends that have the greatest significance and are the most indeterminate (Ratcliffe, 2000).

(6) *Develop coherent scenarios*. Next, pinpoint the precarious factors using Table 6. Categorise them by

Table 5.   Driving Forces and Inhibitors of Change.

	Perspective	Assumptions
E	Ethical	Morals, norms, conduct, principles
S	Social	Values, relationships, language
T	Technical	Reductionism, scientific logic, rationality, solution, quantification, optimisation, designer knows best
O	Organisational	What? Who? When? Why?
P	Political	Small p and big P; issues, interests local, national, global
P	Physical	Environment, conservation, green issues
E	Economic	Production, distribution, demand-supply; actions and interactions of economic agents and how economies work.
L	Legal	Requirements, responsibilities, status

Source: Adapted from Linstone (1984)

Table 6. Properties of Persistent Interests.

(a) Complex	Multiple causes and consequences
	Multi-sector, multi-scale
	Embedded in societal structures and institutions
(b) Uncertain	No 'ready-made' solutions
	Uncertainty cannot be reduced through knowledge acquisition
	interventions primarily alter the interest perception, not the interest itself
(c) Obstacles	Involvement of numerous autonomous factors with diverse interests at multiple scale levels
(d) Hard to grasp	Resist interpretation
	Ill-structured
	Susceptible to power dynamics

Source: Based on Martens and Rotmans (2005).

theme; or causal. Reduce the scenarios to two – four, maximum. Next, develop each scenario so that it is meaningful and potentially real, giving each one a name.

(7) *Pinpoint 1–5 career choices.* This step considers the strategic implications of the task defined in step one within the context of the generated scenarios (Ratcliffe, 2000). This process is achieved by updating, corroborating, filtering, enlarging or eliminating existing solutions and filters. Key decision makers should then select and rank the filters from the most to the least important.

(8) *Evaluate each final scenario.* Use a 5-point Likert scale based on uncertainties, participants' priorities or the likelihood that a participant is more likely to pursue one scenario over others. Total the scores for each scenario and then compare them.

(9) *Delineate the Career Value Chain*

People are central to career value chains, which are formed by prospective employees whose capability will be strongly pursued. To sum it up, the career value chain includes the following:

(a) Productive work: creativity, ability to work in a team, being able to take the initiative.

(b) Remuneration.

(c) Organisation's reputation including products and services.

(d) Workplace culture: values; free from bullying and harassment.

(e) Career development.

(f) Flexible work: amenable to accommodate a worker's caring responsibilities or studies.

These factors, in addition to incentives and fulfilment of undertakings given to employees at the time of recruitment, are also indispensable as is maintaining their initial enthusiasm for the role (Koudelkova & Milichovsky, 2015). Employers need to assure that they attract the most suitable employees and ensure that they can sustain them by supporting their career building. Interests occur when interests and incentives for individuals are misaligned with those of the employer, sometimes because the employer has not fulfilled their part of the employment contract. Failures of this kind result in exploitation of employees, desperate to retain a foothold in the labour market. Mutual exchange and cooperation increase resources of production, capability development, whereas the opposite occurs without it. Cooperation facilitates value for both employers and employees.

Employee engagement leads to high commitment (e.g. loyalty) (Brewer, 1994; Gupta, Joshi, & Agarwal, 2012). Achieving this is vital. Employers need to provide a clear articulation and adoption of ethical and equity principles, what the organisation stands for, how it is positioned in the marketplace and the fit with capability (Starineca, 2016). Organisational commitment is demonstrated by all employees not only by human resources through a respectful social responsibility climate, by providing new employees and reminding existing one with help and support from mentorship, coaching and the like (Lazauskaite-Zabielske, Urbanaviciute, & Bagdziuniene, 2015)

CONCLUSION

Virtual and immersive technologies are now a reality. Through artificial intelligence and the like, it may be possible for people to play a more decisive role in career choice than ever before and also learn about their capability, skill development and outcomes.

Design thinking is a sustainable framework for thinking and strategising towards developing career options. Given the complexity of this topic, design thinking allows participants to engage deeply with the process and provides a sense of achievement as it progresses seeds of an idea to prototyping.

REFERENCES

Amit, R., & Zott, C. (2002). Value drivers of e-commerce business models. In M. A. Hitt, R. Amit, C. Lucier, & R. D. Nixon (Eds.), *Creating value: Winners in the new business environment* (pp. 15–47). Oxford: Blackwell.

Argyris, C. (1985). *Strategy, change and defensive routines.* New York, NY: Harper Business.

Ayrgris, C., & Schön, D. A. (1996). *Organisational learning II.* Reading, MA: Addison-Wesley.

Argyris, C., & Schon, D. (1974). *Theory in practice: Increasing professional effectiveness.* San Francisco: Jossey Bass.

Badke, W. (2012). *Teaching research processes: The faculty role in the development of skilled human researchers.* Oxford: Chandos.

Beetham, R., & Sharpe, H. (2007). *Rethinking pedagogy for a digital age: designing and delivering e-learning.* London: Routledge.

Benson, J., & Dresdow, S. (2014). Design thinking: A fresh approach for transformative assessment practice. *Journal of Management Education, 38,* 436–461.

Bittner, J. V., Bruena, M., & Rietzschel, E. F., (2016). Cooperation goals, regulatory focus, and their combined effects on creativity. *Thinking Skills and Creativity, 19,* 260–268.

Brewer, A. M. (1993). *Managing for employee commitment.* Melbourne, Australia: Longman Professional.

Brown, T. (2008). Design thinking. *Harvard Business Review, 86*(6), 84–92.

City, E. A., Elmore, R. F., Fiarman, S. E., & Teitel, L. (2009). *Instructional rounds in education.* Cambridge, MA: Harvard Education Press.

Cooke, N. J., Kiekel, P. A., & Helm, E. E. (2001). Measuring Team Knowledge During Skill Acquisition of a Complex Task, *International Journal of Cognitive Ergonomics, 5*(3), 297–315.

Curşeu, P. L., & Brink, T. T. (2016). Minority dissent as teamwork related mental model: Implications for willingness to dissent and group creativity. *Thinking Skills and Creativity*, *22*, 86–96.

De Dreu, C. K., Baas, M., & Nijstad, B. A. (2008). Hedonic tone and activation level in the mood-creativity link: Toward a dual pathway to creativity model. *Journal of Personality and Social Psychology*, *94*, 739–756.

Dicle, Ü., & Köse, C. (2014). The Impact of Organizational Learning on Corporate Sustainability and Strategy Formulation with the Moderating Effect of Industry Type, *Procedia-Social and Behavioral Sciences*, *150*, 958–967.

Dweck, C. S. (1996). Implicit theories as organisers of goals and behaviour. In P. M. Gollwitzer, & J. A. Bargh (Eds.), *The psychology of action. Linking cognition and motivation to behaviour* (pp. 69–90). New York, NY: Guildford Press.

Dye, L. D. (2002). 'Using scenario planning as an aid in project portfolio management. In *Proceedings of the Project Management Institute Annual Seminars and Symposium*, October 3–10, San Antonio, TX.

Dym, C. L., Agogino, A., Eris, O., Frey, D., & Leifer, L. (2005). Engineering design thinking, teaching, and learning. *Journal of Engineering Education*, *94*(1), 103–120.

Glen, R., Suciu, C., & Baughn, C. (2014). The need for design thinking in business schools. *Academy of Management Learning & Education*, *13*(4), 653–667.

Goleman, D. (2006). *Social intelligence: The new science of human relationships*. London: Bantam Books.

Gupta, B., Joshi, S., & Agarwal, M. (2012). The effect of expected benefit and perceived cost on employees' knowledge sharing behaviour: A study of it employees in India. *Organisations and Markets in Emerging Economies*, 3(1), 8–19.

Hassi, L., & Laakso, M. (2011). Design thinking in the management discourse: Defining the elements of the concept. Contribution to the 18th International Product Development Management Conference, Innovate Through Design, Delft, the Netherlands.

Hattie, J., & Timperley, H. (2007). The power of feedback. *Review of Educational Research*, 77, 81–112.

Hirst, G., Van Knippenberg, D., Chen, C. H., & Sacramento, C. A. (2011). How does bureaucracy impact individual creativity? A cross-level investigation of team contextual influences on goal orientation-creativity relationships. *Academy of Management Journal*, 54(3), 624–641.

Kelley, T., & Kelley, D. (2013). *Creative confidence: Unleashing the creative potential within us all*. Crown Business Currency.

Kelley, T., & Littman, J. (2001). *The art of innovation: Lessons in creativity from IDEO Americas leading design firm*. New York, NY: Doubleday.

Koh, J., Ching, C., Wong, B., & Huang-Yao, H. (2015). Technological pedagogical content knowledge and design thinking: A framework to support ICT lesson design for 21st century learning. *The Asia-Pacific Education Researcher*, 24(3), 535–543.

Korde, R., & Paulus, P. B. (2017). Alternating individual and group idea generation: fiFinding the elusive synergy. *Journal of Experimental Social Psychology*, 70, 177–190.

Koudelkova, P., & Milichovsky, F. (2015). Successful innovation by motivation. *Business: Theory and Practice*, *16*(3), 223–230.

Lazauskaite-Zabielske, J., Urbanaviciute, I., & Bagdziuniene, D. (2015). The role of prosocial and intrinsic motivation in employees' citizenship behaviour. *Baltic Journal of Management*, *10*(3), 345–365.

Lebuda, I., Galewska-Kustra, M., & Glăveanu, V. P. (2016). Creativity and social interactions. *Creativity Theory and Research Application*, *3*, 187–193.

Lenton, R., Sidhu, R., Kaur, S., Conrad, M., Kennedy, B., et al. (2014). *Community service learning and community-based learning as approaches to enhancing university service learning*. Toronto, Canada: Higher Education Quality Council of Ontario.

Linstone, H. (1984). *Multiple perspectives for decision making: Bridging the gap between analysis and action*. Amsterdam, Netherlands: Elsevier Science Pub. Co.

March, J. G. (1991). Exploration and exploitation in organisational learning. *Organisation Science*, *2*(1), 71–87.

March, J. G., & Olsen, J. P. (1975). The uncertainty of the past: Organizational learning under ambiguity. *European Journal of Political Research*, *3*(2), 147–171.

Martens, P., & Rotmans, J. (2005). Transitions in a globalising world. *Futures*, *37*(10), 1133–1144.

Martin, R. (2007). *The opposable mind*. Harvard: Harvard Business School Press.

Nyhan, B., & Reifler, J. (2010). When corrections fail: The persistence of political misperceptions. *Political Behavior*, *32*, 303–330.

Onora, N. (1975). *Acting on principle: An essay in Kantian ethics*. New York, NY: Columbia University Press.

Osborn, N. (1963). *Applied imagination: Principles and procedures of creative problem solving* (3rd Rev. ed.). New York, NY: Charles Scribner's Sons.

Ramsden, P. (1992). *Learning to teach in higher education*. London: Routledge.

Ratcliffe, J. (2000). Scenario building: A suitable method for strategic property planning. *Property Management*, *18*(2), 127–144.

Roome, N., & Wijen, F. (2006). Stakeholder power and organisational learning in corporate environmental management. *Organisation Studies*, *27*(2), 235–263.

Sarasvathy, S. (2001). Causation and effectuation: Toward a theoretical shift from economic inevitability to entrepreneurial contingency. *Academy of Management Review*, *26*(2), 243–263.

Schon, D. A. (1984). *The reflective practitioner: How professionals think in action*. New York, NY: Basic books.

Simon, H. A. (1969). *The sciences of the artificial*. Cambridge, MA: MIT Press.

Starineca, O. (2016). Human resource selection approaches and socially responsible strategy. *Economics and Business* (28), 106–114.

Thibodeau, P., & Boroditsky, L. (2011). Metaphors we think with: The role of metaphor in reasoning. *PLoS ONE*, *6*, e16782.

Vianna, M., Vianna, Y., Adler, I., Lucena, B., & Russo, B. (2012). *Design thinking: Business innovation*. Rio de Janeiro, Brazil: MVJ Press.

Yeager, D. S., Romero, C., Paunesku, D., Hulleman, C. S., Schneider, B., et al. (2016). Using design thinking to improve psychological interventions: The case of the growth mindset during the transition to high school. *Journal of Educational Psychology*, *108*(3), 374–391.

PART III

PROTOTYPING CAREERS

5

CAREER PROTOTYPING: DESIGNING CAREER THROUGH A SELF-NARRATIVE

INTRODUCTION

Let's revisit the question posed in chapter one: 'what is a career?' For many people, careers present a real conundrum as work and how it is organised, is increasingly dislocated. Some people lament this, while others see it as an opportunity for discovery by generating careers as spaces for new ideas.

Part I of this book focussed on career growth, while Parts II and III focus on both opportunities and disruptive growth. In chapter 2, career thinking was introduced. The focus in this chapter continues that process to assist in understanding how to draw upon the perceptions of others, to experiment, generate alternative career options, collect feedback and design a purposeful career by interrogating one's current skills, unbundling them and re-bundling them.

A career is prototypically an active and self-motivated pursuit. Changing careers is not just a case of moving from one position to another rather a person's self-identity, well-being and capability become vested within and dependent upon it. A person's perspective changes alongside it, so a career change is a process of interchange, an intersection in life or otherwise an integration, a blending of past pathways.

A career change is an investment in one's future, a genuine gain rather than a loss, although this is not always realised at the time. The investment which a person makes in their career is in itself transformative. A career is not a direct correlation between a person's inputs and their outputs, like a balance sheet. Career experiences are not easy as they are a source of personal identity and assessment and sometimes criticism through and by others as well as doubt, adjustment, growth and development.

However, the career process is more important than a simple overview of a person's assets and deliverables. A triggering event (e.g. an overlooked promotion or observing others making career-changing transitions) often spurs a career change and is sometimes accompanied by the forging of a new one.

As stated in Chapter 4, career thinking is a creative process drawing on both emotional and cognitive intelligence as well as a person's observations of others and their views about how others perceive them in the absence of direct feedback. Careers are about people; they are relationally formed, dynamic and open for continuous change and, indeed, disruption. Careers as prototypes attract people to them with yet unrealised skills, enacted in unforeseen contexts and new technologies, giving rise to innovative practice.

Prototyping requires curiosity, imagination and creativity to generate, explore and develop possible solutions, and bestows value on the end user (Howard, 2016). The challenge is to develop a way to elicit opportunities to organise a career that creates value for career incumbents and their associated stakeholders. Bringing to fruition what the incumbent knows to realise their career purpose. For prototyping, there are different emphases, including identify and refine their identity in the context of collaborative career prototyping as well as information needs and resources.

Up until recently, prototyping was utilised mainly by inventors, researchers, technical experts and the like. By the same token, prototyping a career facilitates and energises people to engage in thinking about their potential futures. It is a guided, self-directed learning approach and assists people to design something fit for purpose for themselves. A significant consequence in making career prototypes is the creation of new alignments between people throughout the process, including narrating and demonstrating these new alignments as models for future practice. A prototype converts a notion, a dream into something more concrete and 'engagable'.

Prototyping a career draws on participants' confidence and capacity to mock-up the desired model. It is a process for bringing together both tangible and intangible attributes which leads to skill development, including psychological. Prototyping stimulates creative thinking. Inventing a career is a way for ascribing agency to potential career incumbents. It delivers purpose and belief to career planning that otherwise might be seen as a random happening. Prototyping includes three parts:

1. Stimulating – Envisioning an ideal career.

2. Progressing – What should my career be?

3. Reinforcing – What will my career be?

These three parts will be explored in the following sections.

ENVISIONING AN IDEAL CAREER THROUGH PROTOTYPING

Careers, like prototypes, are either fresh ideas or a melding of the new with 'old' ideas, triggered by a novel situation.

A 'prototype' is unique modelled on something else; an exemplar, an artefact (Simpson & Weiner, 1989). Careers are prototyped using artefacts or stories that 'make a possible future visible' (Turner, 2016, p. 328).

Careers, like archetypes, replicate how people understand their relationships with others, the way they work with others, all of which contributes symbolic meaning for identity creation. Each career has a character of its own evidenced by the stereotypical attributes applied to occupational groupings, for example, occupations such as accountant, engineer, nurse, priest and sales representative predispose-specific stereotypes. Each one is typecast by its cultural, contextual and discipline bases, which often supersede specific national and cultural boundaries. For example, a medical practitioner has a similar status, expectations seen in most industrialised societies.

Prototyping is initiated by a person reflecting on their lived experiences, preferably mediated by a facilitator, so they are recalled, forming insight about future career options. A mediated experience is generated by word-of-mouth narratives about events from everyday life. People are the unconscious designers of their imagination, calling on memory or their immediate experience, rearranging or embellishing these to make sense of what is going on (based on Campbell, 1994). This process is vital in career prototyping.

These formulaic ways of thinking tap into the community's perception, linking the central psychological predispositions of people with specific occupations that they import and integrate as they become an incumbent in an occupational role. The reason for this is that people are primarily identity-seeking. A career is one of the prime vehicles for achieving this. When societies were less challenged by global forces of change than they are today, people followed traditions and largely maintained their parents' views about desired occupations. For example, in some cases, career selection is ritualistic, simply following the family tradition of going into the family business, farm or shop, or the legal, medical or teaching profession or they had a 'calling' in life, that is, a vocation. Rituals bestow advantages, and this is further heightened and perpetuated by myths, and heroes are personifications of this. For example, there are specific auras or myths associated with start-up entrepreneurs, media moguls, actors, forensic scientist or a social activist and so on.

Career Discovery

Igniting people's creative imagination early in the discovery phase gives rise to new ideas and thought structures, not through accumulation by itself rather exponentially by connecting cognitive and affective emotions as previously discussed. Resourceful imaginings work to boost the attachment of meaning and value derived from the direct and indirect experience of various careers in the past. More than just a dream, it sharpens people's focus on career options, leading them, feeling that they are getting somewhere in terms of career direction, as shown in Fig. 1.

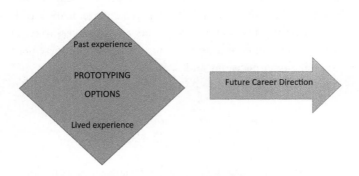

Fig. 1.   Career Discovery through Prototyping.

As previously stated, careers are central to people's lives in terms of utility, symbolism, status and, hence, identity (Miller, 2008). Most people continuously reflect and often share with others about what is going on in their lives. Facebook, Instagram and Twitter are classic examples of this. In designing a career, the sharing of ideas, preferences and suggestions are usually called upon to address important questions such as:

1. What is the purpose and meaning of a career today?

2. Why do some careers feature more prominently in specific contexts and societies while other careers are considered marginal? The significance of careers has altered over time too.

3. Why is it that some people are instantly attracted or have a strong passion with certain careers that often take up a large percentage of their lives, while others treat their careers as far less significant in their life?

A career prototype is a way of organising and demonstrating a future opportunity providing examples to serve as evidence of potential outcomes. While a prototype fabricates the career picture, it seeks to depict reality. It is created at the end of a line of investigation to create an ideal version based on the discovery and development phase. Career prototypes are ideal ways for participants and observers to tease out their elements and ascertaining value and endorsement for their career decisions and actions.

Progressing the Career Prototype: What Should a Career Be?

A narrative is an ideal method to materialise a person's internalised, career story that serves to integrate past, present and prospective career accounts. The stories or narratives are used to help express life themes and interpret future work and career ideas. It is this story that forges the career direction as depicted in Fig. 1. Further, through this process, identity is formed. It is a dialogical development process including internal dialogues that people have continuously such as self-talk when a person is trying to address their misgivings, missteps, misapprehensions, trust and distrust as well as how knowledge is produced in design thinking among participants. People from all backgrounds tell and retell stories to themselves, each other, listen to others' stories and pass them on and through this process, establish notions of self, social and cultural identities which influences them in diverse ways at various stages of their careers (Eckhardt & Houston, 2002).

Narratives take diverse forms: big picture story, relationship story, calamity story, inner story, each one showing chronology, people that are important to the person, values, beliefs, interests, emotions, conflicts and climates. This four part model helps a person to understand how a career builds and can work its way around a narrative to potentially provide a greater understanding of the big picture or conversely the inner narrative, for example. This approach provides a more powerful lens for understanding how career impacts positively or negatively on someone's well-being. When looked at in conjunction with the archetypes (see next section) this facilitates a deeper understanding of career aspirants and why their lived or mediated experiences of careers are as they are. The narrative method indicates a person's ideas, psychosocial and physical preferences in terms of work.

Another helpful tool is the use of universal archetypes, such as those outlined by Jung (1948). Some archetypes, according to Jung (1948) guide people about how to create and structure a career for themselves through innovation and entrepreneurship drawing on archetypes such as creator; others focus on service such as a caregiver. Others archetypes depict different career stories such as explorer and navigator. Some people relish the opportunity of connecting with people in a significant way such as an entertainer or leader, and others want to leave their mark on the world, for example, a politician, a religious group or disrupt the status quo.

Prototyping can kick off by addressing the following:

Identifying Career Gaps in the Market – What Is Missing in the Career Market Place Today?

(a) What expectations need to be true to realise your career?

(b) Does the person need to give up or arrange certain things for career preparation, and are they willing to do so?

(c) Request the person to provide a story narrative for their career expectations.

Innovating – What Would a Career Look Like If Participants

(a) query the attributes of selected careers;

(b) convert their career vision into something more specific;

(c) integrate their ideas and explain them to others; and

(d) role-play selected scenarios to bring some reality to career experience.

Translating Ideas into Outcomes

Prototyping is an integral part of converting non-tangible ideas or theory into practice (Boni, Weingart, & Evenson, 2009). It is a way of translating ideas into real-world outcomes through a process of experimentation, such as an invention. Inventing or innovating is continuously refining the learning gleaned through collaboration with others as well as considering other inputs, the essence of the prototyping process. Prototyping allows people to identify improvements for future trials and potential solutions (Brown, 2008).

Consequently, prototyping is incremental and shaped by trial and error as well as envisioning and representing the outcome or the solution to the initial problem (Glen, Suciu, & Baughn, 2014; Hassi & Laakso, 2011). For example, in this case, it is the career outcome that a person is seeking. Prototyping can take the form of diagrams, photos, models, graphs, stories and other ways to design outcomes to define it instead of writing a report, for instance.

DIVERGENT AND CONVERGENT THINKING

Prototyping cycles through the process of divergent thinking (comprehensive, bearing in mind multiple options) towards convergent thinking (tapering, filtering down to one or two paramount options). The next step is to recycle back to broader thinking if the narrowing has occurred without an optimal focus.

As previously stated, prototyping is an iterative development of investigating a problem or a question and trialling ways to solve it. The outcome is by people applying their thinking, engaging in the issue, asking questions and applying the feedback advantageously.

The more 'finished' a prototype seems the less likely its creators will be able to pay attention to and profit from feedback. The goal of prototyping is to learn about the strengths and weaknesses of the idea and to identify new directions that further prototypes might take. (Brown, 2008, p. 3)

In the case of career thinking, the approach to take involves a career model. Developing a career model is thinking about a career as a product or a service which a person is seeking to improve upon (based on Osterwalder & Pigneur, 2010). A career model has various constituent components which need to be investigated (based on Trimi & Berbegal-Mirabent, 2012).

LEARNING THEORY AND COLLABORATIVE CAREER BUILDING

Collaborative career-building requires a team to design an overarching vision and its components, including prospective experience, people, work networks, worksites and so on. When the group reaches a consensus about the broad design, each participant then begins developing their unique vision, including the prospective experience, people, networks, worksites and things that occupy this career space. An individual vision is aligned with the collaboratively conceptualised notion of their particular career focus. The collection of individual visions expands the participants' understanding of the career they have designed. Each person then continues to refine it by augmenting and revising the overarching concept. In this way, the individual vision of career continuously progresses.

Examining career through diverse personal visions is similar to *constructivist* learning theory based on Piaget (1954). Constructivism posits that people internalise how careers work even if they have little or no direct experience. People obtain such views from the media (books, television, films and games) as well as in their relationships (interactions with parents, peers, teachers, co-people, etc.). From early childhood, these career 'models' are acted out and create narratives about what careers young people may pursue as adults. These imaginary models and insights from media, etc., assist people in formulating and building their career plans. Prototyping is similar and allows participants to continue a dialogue with themselves and others to grapple with the specifics and address discrepancies while also continually rethinking and readjusting their viewpoints and opinions based on the feedback. Prototyping allows for encouraging discussions. Participants move between critical thinking and creative production, back and forth and back again, where the two become so intertwined that it is difficult to distinguish one from the other. Thinking and making are not separate activities but part of a whole. A collaborative project begins as a blank canvas that participants complete. Participants usually begin hesitantly, not sure if they are doing things the 'right way' and not wishing to step on anyone else's toes with their creations. With guidance and support, prototyping takes shape by perceiving links among its various components.

Career Coaching Exercise

1. Drawing on a fictional case study, ask yourself, what is most important for you?

2. Conduct a mentoring session with someone in a career transition.

3. Conduct a similar conversation with a colleague in the workplace and discuss aspects that are potentially conflicting and complementary.

4. Compare the outcomes. Think about the influence of
    your partner in conversation while looking for personal
    aspects of yourself.

    a. Describe situations which are energising, for
        example, engaging in activity that you are
        passionate about – sport, art, cooking, walking,
        playing with a pet.

    b. What was the outcome? Describe and explain this.

5. Anticipate how you may replicate this passion at work.

DEVELOPING A CAREER CLINIC FOR CAREER PROTOTYPING

Career designers such as career mentors, coaches, counsellors, guidance officer assist individuals shape, review and
navigate a career plan or journey as they transition from
one position to the next. The duration of the first meeting is
approximately 90 minutes and includes some guided questions about specific elements of the people experience (i.e.
divergent stage).

Encourage fluid conversation, keeping track of themes,
sub-themes and open dialogue.

The examination of the opus is now in-depth to test some
career concepts. Core questions include elements of usabil-
ity (e.g. Does the logic of the opus make sense? What would
some of the challenges be in using this tool?), scope (e.g. Is
there missing or extraneous content?), context (e.g. In what
types of careers or career development contexts would this
tool be most effective? To whom would it be most useful?)
and contribution (e.g. How does this compare with existing
tools or frameworks in the education literatures?).

PROTOTYPING WORKSHOP

A workshop for employers, career designers and prospective people to work in groups of two to four using the opus to map out an actual experiential career that they were planning or realising within their enterprise.. During the concluding debrief, solicit detailed feedback from the participants about their experience with the opus.

A CAREER OPUS FRAMEWORK

Both the development and application of a career opus is an example of a prototype. In this case, the opus is a framework for a person to use to design a career or a pathway in a way that is not too dissimilar to the process that composers use to create a piece of music, a writer a novel or an artist a visual work. It is a way to bring a person's imagination to life.

Career Opus Defined

A career opus provides an organising, planning and reviewing dais as a reference point through all stages of the process from idea generation to implementation, followed by reflective gap analysis as well as a post hoc evaluation of the outcome. The opus is created by applying the prototyping philosophy of decisively and expressively connecting with the development process either alone or in collaboration with others. Similarly, it directs people through the process of applying prototyping principles in their career development. In the next section, the method to create a career opus, that is, prototyping and its constituent features and how these are employed. Value propositions (co-created benefits), to which all other elements connect. While this arrangement implies a coherence within the opus, it is neither rigid nor undeviating. The career opus is organic and iterative: it facilitates viewing the parts as well as the whole, facilitating easy navigation between ideas and examining diverse, career scenarios. The career opus and components apply to all career contexts, and it is a good substitute for a career 'business case'. The various components of a career opus include the following:

(a) Vision

(b) Values

(c) Design features

(d) Career substance

(e) Stakeholders shaping careers

(f) Networking relationships for building careers

(g) Communications for career-making

(h) Resources for designing a career

(i) Career activities

(j) Career outcomes and impacts

(k) Limitations for career design

CAREER VISION

Career objectives or developing a 'vision' for a career are indispensable for making a case for a career whether applying for a position or choosing a divergent path, for example, start-up. How do people gain a firm(er) grasp on these abstract dimensions of meaning for career designing and seeking?

One way to address this is to employ metaphors, as discussed in Chapter 3. This process is achieved by exercising

Morgan's (1986) method of 'multiple metaphors', for example. Using this frame, the facilitator asks: what are the key metaphors for careers, which allow people to consider potential opportunities?

A career journey: allows a person to pick up at any point in their career path so far and to discuss their aims, aspirations or equally, their frustrations and disappointments. It also allows participants to consider what might be the next steps.

A career tree is also a useful metaphor for people to consider in terms of branching out or aiming higher or taking the opportunity to choose from the lower branches.

The notion of a family career allows people to discuss expectations: past and present with family members engaged in a business,; whether they are considering entering the family business or following in the footsteps of a family member's career.

A fit for purpose metaphor raises issues of capability both acquired and inherited (e.g. physical attributes for being a professional sports career), personal and occupational change, and whether the fit is achieved by matching people to positions or positions to people.

Career growth leads to a discussion about the catalysts for career development and explicitly acknowledges as a primary goal the continuous development of the individual and the expression of their potential. A discussion about mentoring or coaching is relevant here.

Creative career design focusses on building one's career. Some people measure their careers by accomplishments or works completed, even those who do not often consider the career itself as something they have created. In the current career environment, careers are less likely to be planned and more likely to be flexible or improvised as a person moves forward in their journey. What are the implications of considering ourselves as the artists and crafters of our own lives?

Network careers might be considered as co-operative collectives. Each career combines with other careers to create goods and services for society. The organisational perspective, mainstream in business schools and in business management, sets the economic welfare of the organisation ahead of all other goals. Organisations achieve goals through the skilful acquisition, combination and management of human resources. The phrase 'human resource management' is a metaphor that potentially appropriates and transforms individual knowledge capital for organisational purposes, reduces people to inert substances and entrusts careers to the superior knowledge of the company. Practices such as corporate career workshops, assessment centres, training, development programmes and performance appraisal provide opportunities for career development but leave open the question of career ownership as between individual and organisation. Moreover, all career protagonists are potentially at risk of unconscious capture by the organisation's rhetoric of resources and commitment, to the possible long-term detriment of their careers. They and their advisors need to understand this metaphor, its rhetoric, its potential benefits and its dangers.

PERSONAL CAREER VALUES

Values are advantageous benchmarks that are constant regardless of context, although they may vary in importance depending on the situation (Schwartz, 1992). Examples include creativity, equality, fairness, diversity and fidelity. As abstract notions, values are interpreted in various ways, and this shapes how they motivate and guide actions (Maio, 2016) as ways to defend or clarify attitudes, decisions and actions. A universal values model proposed by Schwartz et al. (2012) based on 57 values, used 10-value categories across four dimensions including openness to change (e.g. autonomy) versus conservation (e.g. status quo) and self-enhancement (e.g. ambition) versus self-transcendence (e.g. social justice). This model demonstrates how different values drive different goals and outcomes depending on which values people prioritise in their lives.

Identifying a personal set of values provides an understanding of the person-role and person-career fit and how this shapes their cultural fit and ultimately impact their achievement and performance in specific contexts. For example, people who like to serve others are likely to have a somewhat different value set compared to those who do not. It is important to understand that in thinking about future roles and careers. Most people understand this instinctively; however, it is important for designing a career to deliberate on personal value sets and to compare this to both the occupational as well as potential employer values. How values are conceptualised and articulated and how they are enacted are quite distinct.

What are your core career values – those things that guide what a life course?

Neither career objectives nor vision will articulate the 'design case' for a new idea in a similar way to value propositions.

VALUE PROPOSITIONS FOR CAREER PEOPLE AND DESIGNERS

Value propositions are worthwhile for career people and designers alike in the same way that anyone purchasing a service or product needs to understand both its inherent and extrinsic value. Whereas career objectives are directly aligned with the value propositions and are an important part of informing the value proposition to students in particular. Value propositions are the starting place and core of a career opus as they anchor all other elements. Consider the following questions to assist this process:

1. What value will this career create overall?

2. What value will this career deliver (i.e. what does it offer) to each partner or stakeholder?

3. What needs will this career fill? Why is it a good idea?

Value propositions encompass a broader conceptualisation of benefits and outcomes, and they also consider more than just one stakeholder. Given that there are multiple constituents to whom a career provides value, there is more than one value proposition to consider. Value propositions demonstrate the reasons why a career is a good idea and its anticipated benefits.

COLLABORATIVE AND INDIVIDUAL CAREER CO-DESIGNING

Career prototypes are developed in a workshop with others, with the group members taking it, in turn, to work on one person's story at a time. Co-designing has benefits for both individuals and groups working together on joint task as it produces knowledge and wisdom.

The process is initiated by a macro, prospective analysis to enable group members to address questions and issues relating to future careers using one or more of the following methods:

a) Smart speculations – How will this change in the future? Success concerns the person who achieves goals and compares their actions to those of others.

b) Occupational analysis – what are the skills, knowledge and attributes required.

c) Identifying gaps in the market – what is missing in the market place today?

   I. What expectations need to be true to realise your career?

   II. Does the aspirant need to give up or arrange certain things for career preparation, and are they willing to do so?

   III. Request the aspirant to provide a story narrative for their career expectations.

d) Innovation – what would a career look like if

   I. the career person questioned their assumptions;

   II. converted their career vision into something more specific;

   III. integrate their ideas and explain them to others; and

   IV. role-playing scenarios will assist in making it more real, so they can experience what some of the career aspects might be like in reality.

e) After designing the prototype, compare it to the current career options and align these to the expected outcome dimensions. Who are their competitors? How do career portfolios compare?

Occupational Analysis – Career Skills,
Knowledge and Attributes.

Exploring a Personal Profile: Career Strengths and Skills
Continuities

(a) What's the career person's influence plan?

(b) Thinking across a range of past situations, what do
    others frequently commend?

(c) If given a choice, what tasks or roles would you seek
    out at work?

(d) How do others always describe you – think about how
    the career person's supervisor or friend introduces them
    to others?

(e) What triggers you into action? What demotivates you
    at work?

(f) What is the most important achievement you have
    attained to date?

(g) In considering the above which ones will be the most
    significant for the career person in a future role?

*Now list three key points, say three to five words that best
describe you.*

CAREER STRENGTHS AND SKILL GAPS

What skills do people need to strengthen? Why? Use the
following list to develop this (Table 1).

List three key points in three to five areas for strengthening.
Set a deadline for achieving this in the next six to 12 months.
How will progress be monitored to ensure achievement? Use
Table 2 to draft this.

Table 1.   Career Prototypes.

Core Values	Skills	Context
Freedom	*Personal skills*	*Action orientation*
Equality	a. Dependability	a. Physical
Pleasure	b. Accountability	b. Mental
Security	c. Self-management	c. Combination of
Equality	d. Emotional	mental and physical
Social justice	intelligence	d. Interactive
Diversity	e. Independent	e. Self-focused
Public service	f. Confidence	
Conservative	g. Openness to new	
Liberal	ideas and learning	
Radical	h. Composed	
Learning		
	Critical skills	*Working with people*
	a. Initiating	0–5 children
	b. Prioritising	6–12 years
	c. Problem solving	13–25 years
	d. Numerical	>26 years
	e. Verbal	*Career Stage*
	f. Analytical	a. Early career
		b. Mid-career
		c. Late-career
		d. Elderly
	Discovery skills	*Organisational*
	a. Categorising	a. Private enterprise
	b. Collecting	b. Start-up
	c. Interpreting	c. Small business
	d. Measuring	d. SME
	e. Trialling	e. Partnership
	f. Concluding	f. Public enterprise
		g. NFP
	Communication skills	*Location*
	a. Active listening	a. Outdoors
	b. Demonstrating	b. Indoors
	c. Building	c. National
	relationships	d. International
	d. Collaborating	e. Rural
	e. Serving	f. Metropolitan
	f. Community	
	engagement	
	g. Consulting	
	h. Cultivating donors	

Table 1. *(Continued)*

Core Values	Skills	Context
	i. Diplomatic	
	j. Discrete	
	k. Influencing others	
	l. Instructing	
	m. Leading	
	n. Presenting	
	o. Promoting	
	p. Programming	
	q. Publicising	
	Administrative skills	
	a. Purchasing	
	b. selling	
	c. Financial	
	d. Budgeting	
	e. Organising	
	f. Co-operating	
	g. Strategising	
	h. Co-ordinating tasks, change	
	i. Project management	
	j. Curating information	
	k. Scoping projects	
	l. Writing proposals and reports	
	m. Governing	
	n. Mobilising others	

Table 2. Career Project Report.

Skill Area	Timeline	Milestone

Create an inventory of dissimilar careers and specify their skills and values.

From here develop one career prototype or more, outline the purpose of each one, anticipated outcomes, the occupational context and who are the key stakeholders.

In Step 2, participants develop a set of concepts representing how are these careers likely to be shaped in five to 10 years, and after that, the next 11–20 years.

Participants can use this step to consult with others about how these selected careers may change in the future. Consider the diverse skills and values for these new careers in the future.

In Step 3, each participant based on the perceptions received during their stakeholder collaboration, selected only one concept among those previously defined. They then develop it into a career prototype together with their professional persona and sketch out further by elaborating the details and specifying its characteristics. It is important that participants draw on their experience, knowledge and insights from the first two steps to achieve this. Conduct this exercise through the definition of a usage scenario, in which they describe preparatory steps, skill development and actions which would occur in the course of this career prototype. Seed the scenario by focussing by from now to the next five years, and then the next 6-10 years, depending on the starting point and a person's readiness. Explain how the fictional prototypes are used in the participants' career preparation and choice. This method was selected to assist participants think about their careers in a practical sense, including consequences, as well as to introduce them to the benefits of story-telling as part of design preparation.

In the fourth phase, participants envisage a more distant future and their draft opus of the previous steps to accommodate that vision. Participants apply the following questions: How will I benefit from this new career prototype? What contribution will it make to society? How will it affect me, and how will it change my actions, attitudes and values? Develop each prototype in the form of a narrative using the following storyline prompts, as shown in Table 3

Table 3. Storyline Prompts.

a. Context
b. Purpose
c. What am I feeling, thinking, saying, doing?
d. Where could I observe this type of work, role, task?
e. Is this outcome expected?

Participants are asked to complete their stories and consider how and when they might call upon to use them.

In the final step, participants choose up to three preferred
careers and evaluate their readiness to enter each one, based
on their current skill and value sets. Participants are requested
to consider themselves at the point of retirement and to depict
themselves. What would they have achieved in this career?
Position, money, other? What involvement would they have
made to the 'family unit', community or wider society? Who
would remember them and why? What influence would participants have made on the actions, attitudes and values?

OUTCOMES OF THE PROTOTYPING PROCESS

The level of engagement with the opus at each stage is marked.
Participants are encouraged to experiment with it and to test
their ideas. During each phase, people are encouraged to provide feedback and reshape as they see fit.

As each group revises their prototype ranging from minor
wordsmithing to substantive revisions, the different stakeholder groups experimented with the opus and applied it to their
context. Gradually the needs and preferences of the groups
begin to converge as people make continuous adjustments.

People create guiding questions for each block of the
opus. People add arrows and shading to show general move-
ment and connection among the ideas, ensuring that they

understand that there is no 'right' or 'wrong' way to approach it, nor is any element of the prototype that is static or permanent. In all, people create multiple versions of a career opus, each being thoroughly examined and manipulated by its potential (divergent approach) before arriving at a template that optimises peoples' needs (convergent approach) until they formulate a pre-prototype as shown in Fig. 2.

As participants work through these stages, they will clarify goals, drawing on their back story, feelings and sort out any incongruences. Sometimes people start to modify their perspectives and focus on their positive attributes rather than their negative ones. They enjoy answering the questions and focussing on themselves in what they see as professional prototyping and engage in the process enthusiastically leading to learning a new skill.

A prototyping process is the sequence of six steps or activities which a person employs to conceive, design and action a career plan. This development process typically includes the following activities as seen in Fig. 3: identifying a person's career needs, establishing aims, concept generation, concept selection,

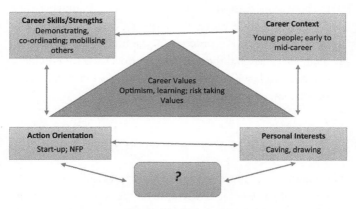

Fig. 2.   An Example of Working towards a Career Pre-prototype.

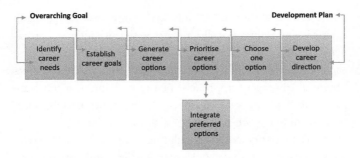

Fig. 3.   An Example of Working towards a Career Prototype.

concept testing, reviewing a plan, setting priorities and action. In the process, various ideas are introduced and evaluated in terms of the criteria (i.e. the highest benefit vs. the lowest investment). This ideation phase is key to what follows as it governs the course of developing the exemplar. After this stage has been accepted, the design process will diverge towards a comprehensive solution. Selecting the best exemplar to prototype is also essential. The capacity to assess design ideas, throughout their development within the design process, is an indispensable part of the goal to increase value. The activity of mediating between and selecting from a range of competing exemplar options is a significant evaluation process. As the number of options to evaluate increases and the available time decreases, it is evident that some people will require high level support in selecting the most satisfying alternative to prototype.

CAREER SPECIALISTS SHAPE CAREERS

Participants are those people who strategically or operationally influence careers or employability outcomes such as employers, employer representatives, educators, students and so on. Stakeholders are important sources of networking too.

Not all participants are engaged in shaping the career opus initially hence the non-linear approach as people may touch base at varying times with influential stakeholders and not always the same people. Stakeholders need to understand the participant's needs, when to sponsor, coach or mentor them or when they may need career guidance.

NETWORKING RELATIONSHIPS FOR BUILDING CAREERS

1. Which relationships have I established?

2. What initiatives are needed to engage stakeholders?

3. How are these relationships interlinked?

For work-integrated learning strategies, reciprocity is a core principle, such that all people (i.e. institutions, students and communities) are equal participants engaged in a democratic process – 'people should both teach and learn' (Lowery et al., 2006, p. 53). Reciprocity needs to be evident throughout the opus. Implementation of careers that involve partnerships by definition involves serving the needs of stakeholders. The opus highlights that building these relationships is part of an intentional career planning process.

COMMUNICATION PROCESSES

1. How can communication be assured?

2. What contextual factors need to be considered?

3. What response mechanisms are required?

Specifying the information required is vital for success (Tryon, Hilgendorf, & Scott, 2009).

PROJECT AND SUBSTANCE

1. How will the project and its elements equate with the value proposals?

2. How will stakeholders be engaged with the learners in the learning process?

3. How will the career be structured, and what learning activities will be employed (e.g. lectures, self-directed learning, video, research, consulting, etc.)?

4. What processes are applied to ensure the quality of outcomes and feedback mechanisms for stakeholders?

Experiential careers present unique learning contexts and development opportunities and require unique career design considerations. People assert that such factors are an essential part of designing a career, particularly when it involves partnerships.

The partners' needs, realities and voice need to be well considered (Stoecker & Tryon, 2009). Tensions can emerge associated with diverse demands, values, misunderstandings and power struggles (Lowery et al., 2006). The value propositions for partners indicate expected outcomes that people are expected to produce – ideally, this too should be developed through a process of co-created with others to specify what is required. These a priori discussions should increase alignment of perspectives and serve to manage expectations regarding what peoples are expected to achieve or produce, as well as facilitate better communication.

Second, the career design needs to reflect accountability to stakeholders, and in particular to partners. For example, what checks and balances will be employed throughout to safeguard that the work is being performed according to expectations? What opportunities will be provided for feedback and mentorship for people regarding their work and conduct, and to support them? How will the career coach ensure that the outcome meets the desired quality standard?

CONSEQUENCES AND INFLUENCES

1. What are the preferred outcomes and influences?

2. What impact did the career have, and how will I know if it is successful?

3. Considerations include learning objectives: aptitude and relationship building, maintenance, accountability and so on.

Individual learning demonstrates knowledge and skills transfer, and also serves as an encouragement for participants to 'engage more deeply and at a higher level' (Biggs & Tang, 2011), rather than just reiterating content (Lenton et al., 2014). The career opus can serve to forge relationships with potential employers as partners in the co-design relationship, thereby home growing the incumbents.

RESOURCES

1. What resources will be required to meet the proposed value?

2. What are the skills, aptitudes and expectations of those involved?

Work-integrated learning is a good example of this although it can lead to inadvertent burdens for employers and in so doing, jeopardise participant outcomes, essential for collaboration, specifying future expectations, training and development (Gonzalez & Golden, 2009).

This is yet again similar to the entrepreneur's rationality who thinks through multiple possibilities, especially when resources are scarce. The educational entrepreneur, like the business entrepreneur, needs to make decisions recurrently based on a cost–benefit analysis, including the imperceptible cost and benefits for all stakeholders. A career opus helps participants to tack through this complexity by linking the resources to the original value proposals. This process is based on reasoning similar to that of Kaplan and Norton's (2001) strategy maps, shaped by decisive processes required to be enhanced to deliver the value proposition promised to customers. There is more than one value proposition, reflecting many stakeholders with different needs, hence the importance of determining what is needed and for which stakeholders for the career opus.

LIMITATIONS

1. What are the boundary conditions for working (e.g. time, policy, culture and structures)?

2. What challenges or considerations are there?

3. What are the underlying assumptions which may prove to be false?

More often than not, those charged with the responsibility of formal career coaching are not used to designing new or innovative, career approaches. Prototyping philosophy often portrays constraints as a source of 'challenge and excitement' that inspires more creative solutions or as a natural part of the exploration process (Dunne & Martin, 2006). Constraints need to be identified, such as the existing job and resource demands and other pressures, faced by the co-designers.

The opus provides a space to investigate creative means of navigating barriers and boundary conditions while understanding and innovating within any immovable parameters.

ACTIVITIES

1. What activities are required to fulfil the value propositions to each stakeholder?

2. What activities lead to collaborative conversations with others?

3. What activities lead to the implementation of a career?

The activities portion of the opus is a plan stating what is significant and what is not and steps towards implementation. A career opus facilitates this process by promoting the dissection of large initiatives into smaller activities, much like goal setting. Enunciating stages towards the end state provides a focussed perspective of the future and is preferable than trying to accomplish radical change (Miller & Wilson, 2006). The opus of each participant guides the instructor to consider those incremental activities that are needed to fulfil the value propositions and implementation. By targeting the activities as a defined component, the opus simplifies by developing 'SMART' goals, that is, specific, measurable, assignable, realistic, time-related (Doran, 1981) and planning that helps the career design coach express what needs to be done to bring value to various stakeholders. Like the other elements in the opus, there is a step-wise action plan to ensure that progress is made. In essence, participants need to consider 'what do we need to activate' and align this to the reasons for doing this; including how will it be implemented and what value it will deliver.

POST-PROTOTYPE CAREER DESIGN

After designing the prototype, compare it to the current career options and align these to the expected outcome dimensions. Who are their competitors?

One further exercise:

Step 1: Imagine you are commissioned to investigate and describe a career of your choosing. To help you consider some potential sources for your career, consider the following:

(a) people who are currently working in this career;

(b) a person who teaches in the area;

(c) people who are considering this career; and

(d) yourself.

Now, consider a career that you would like to do yourself

Step 2: Address the following questions to explain this work, role or career.

(a) What are the key things that stand out in your role?

(b) Why did you choose this career? Did it meet your expectations? Why or why not?

(c) What is the latest trend in this career field? What is the nature of this? What impact has it had so far?

(d) What surprised in your role?

(e) What is the glimpse of wisdom you could offer people thinking about your career?

(f) Anything important that I might have missed?

(g) Anyone else to contact?

Step 3: Create an intranet and ask others (e.g. students, members of professional associations) to post their stories linking them by theme rather than career category.

Step 4: Linking them by theme allows people to see things that they might not see if the careers are classified by category.

CONCLUSION

People develop a career opus using principles of prototyping. A career opus uniquely bridges principles from entrepreneurial business models and experiential learning to provide a platform for instructors, career developers and administrators to engage in innovation and implementation of experiential careers or programmes – particularly those that involve community or organisational partnerships. By adopting a person - centred, collaborative and well-rounded approach from prototyping logic, people have sought to make the opus stimulate a creative process and ongoing stakeholder engagement that will generate and implement mutually beneficial career innovations in a complex and dynamic context.

REFERENCES

Biggs, J. B., & Tang, C. S. (2011). *Teaching for quality learning at university: What the student does.* Maidenhead: Open University Press.

Boni, A. A., Weingart, L. R., & Evenson, S. (2009). Innovation in an academic setting: Designing and leading a business through market-focused, interdisciplinary teams. *Academy of Management Learning and Education, 8*, 407–417.

Brown, T. (2008). Design thinking. *Harvard Business Review*, *86*(6): 84–92.

Campbell, C. (1994). Consuming goods and the goods of consuming. *Critical Review*, *8*(4), 503–520.

Doran, G. T. (1981). There's a S.M.A.R.T. way to write management's goals and objectives. *Management Review, AMA Forum*, *70*, 35–36.

Dunne, D., & Martin, R. (2006). Design thinking and how it will change management education: An interview and discussion. *Academy of Management Learning and Education*, *5*, 512–523.

Eckhardt, G. M., & Houston, M. J. (2002). Cultural psychology and its significance to consumer: Investigating archetype-icon transformation research.*Asia Pacific Advances in Consumer Research*, *5*, 291–292.

Glen, R., Suciu, C., & Baughn, C. (2014). The need for design thinking in business schools. *Academy of Management Learning and Education*, *13*, 653–667.

Gonzalez, J., & Golden, B. (2009). Managing service learners. In R. Stoecker & E. A. Tryon (Eds.), *The unheard voices: Community organisations and service learning* (pp. 73–95). Philadelphia, PA: Temple University Press.

Hassi, L., & Laakso, M. (2011). Making sense of design thinking. In T. M. Karjalainen & M. Salimaki (Eds.), *International design business management papers* (Vol. 1, pp. 50–63). Helsinki, Finland: IDBM Program, Aalto University.

Howard, J. H. (2016). Securing Australia's future? Capabilities for Australian enterprise innovation: The role of government industry and education and research institutions in developing innovation capabilities. Australian Council of

Learned Acadamies. Retrieved from https://www.acola.org.au/PDF/SAF10/Howard.pdf

Jung, C. G. (1948). *The phenomenology of the spirit in fairy tales. The archetypes and the collective unconscious* (Vol. 9(Part 1), pp. 207–254). Princeton, NJ: Princeton University Press.

Kaplan, R. S., & Norton, D. P. (2001). *The strategy-focused organisation: How balanced scorecard companies thrive in the new business environment.* Boston, MA: Harvard Business School Press.

Lenton, R., Sidhu, R., Kaur, S., Conrad, M., Kennedy, B., Munro, Y., & Smith, R. (2014). *Community service learning and community-based learning as approaches to enhancing university service learning.* Toronto, ON: Higher Education Quality Council of Ontario.

Lowery, D., May, D. L., Duchane, K. A., Coulter-Kern, R., Bryant, D., Morris, P. V., Pomery, J. G., & Bellner, M. (2006). A logic model of service-learning: Tensions and issues for further consideration. *Michigan Journal of Community Service Learning, 12*(2), 47–60.

Maio, G. R. (2016). *The psychology of human values.* London: Psychology Press.

Miller, A. D. (2008). Group identification. *Games and Economic Behaviour, 63*(1), 188–202.

Miller, S. J., & Wilson, D. C. (2006). Perspectives on organisational decision making. In S. R. Clegg, C. Hardy, T. Lawrence, & W. R. Nord (Eds.), *Sage handbook of organisation studies* (pp. 469–484). Thousand Oaks, CA: Sage.

Morgan, G. (1986). *Images of organisation* (Exec. Ed.). Thousand Oaks, CA: Sage.

Osterwalder, A., & Pigneur, Y. (2010). *Business model generation: A handbook for visionaries, game changers, and challengers*. Hoboken, NJ: Wiley.

Piaget, J. (1954). *The construction of reality in the child* (Vol. 82). London: Routledge.

Schwartz, S. H. (1992). Universals in the content and structure of values: Theo-retical advances and empirical tests in 20 countries. M. En Zanna (Ed.), *Advances in experimental social psychology* (Vol. 25, pp. 1–65). Berkeley, CA: Academic Press.

Schwartz, S. H., Cieciuch, J., Vecchione, M., Davidov, E., Fischer, R., Beierlein, C., & Konty, M. (2012). Refining theory of basic individual values. *Journal of Personality and Social Psychology*, *103*, 663–688.

Simpson, J. A., & Weiner, E. S. C. (1989). *The Oxford English dictionary* (2nd ed./prepared by J. A. Simpson & E. S. C. Weiner). Oxford: Clarendon Press.

Stoecker, R., & Tryon, E. A. (2009). *The unheard voices: Community organisations and service learning*. Philadelphia, PA: Temple University Press.

Trimi, S., & Berbegal-Mirabent, J. (2012). Business model innovation in entrepreneurship. *International Entrepreneurship and Management Journal*, *8*, 449–465.

Tryon, E., Hilgendorf, A., & Scott, I. (2009). The heart of partnership: Communication and relationships. In R. Stoecker & E. A. Tryon (Eds.), *The unheard voices: Community organisations and service learning* (pp. 96–115). Philadelphia, PA: Temple University Press.

Turner, F. (2016). Prototype. In B. Peters (Ed.), *Digital keywords: A vocabulary of information society and culture* (pp.256–268). Princeton, NJ: Princeton University Press.

6

CAREERS AND CORPORATE SOCIAL RESPONSIBILITY: QUESTIONS AND A CONCLUDING NOTE

INTRODUCTION

Careers single out lives and shape ways of life in profound ways. Is this matched by strategic thinking of government and particularly employers? If so, more young people today will have multiple careers in diverse industries. Are governments and businesses planning for this reality?

Careers are shaped by systemic factors and, therefore, are amenable to change and extinction as these forces disrupt business processes over the last few decades. Employers have gradually exempted themselves from taking responsibility for shaping career pathways as technology disrupts business activities. People no longer start in an organisation following graduation and retire from the same employer at retirement age.

Career making is now the responsibility of individuals, that is, a protean career.

> *The protean career is a process which the person,*
> *not the organization, is managing ... The protean*
> *person's own personal career choices and search*
> *for self-fulfilment are the unifying or integrative*
> *elements in his or her life. The criterion of success*
> *is internal (psychological success), not external.*
> *.........shaped more by the individual than by the*
> *organisation. (Hall & Mirvis, 1995, p. 271)*

The economic welfare of the organisation is privileged ahead of all other goals. Human resource management is a strategy that potentially appropriates and transforms individual knowledge capital for business purposes. Both strategies are within the rights of the employer. However, in order to achieve sustainable economic growth, employers rely on the skilful acquisition, combination and management of employees. Practices such as corporate career workshops, assessment centres, training, development programmes and performance appraisal provide opportunities for career development, without any guarantees to employees for career progression.

Due to the disruptive nature of the economy in every sense and its implications for career, the aspect of corporate social responsibility (CSR) becomes extremely important, as the unsettling influence on the surrounding world is irreversible. Issues related to the sustainable development of employment and career are both local and global concerns. The main idea of CSR for careers is its preservation for future generations. Hence, career thinking is regarded as an investment in the future of society.

At the personal level, work is one of the most important activities for people. At the level of society, work influences a large part of most people's lives, including economic, social, cultural, political and environmental aspects. Is it time for employers to promote sustainable development in the design and construction of employment and careers, by underscoring the importance of careers for people? Is it also time to examine the exploitation of workers, linked to CSR?

As in Chapter 1, the main objective in this chapter is to question the sustainability of careers and indicate how in times of change, the development of advanced technologies and digitisation, the future if not bleak, is causing concern. How can society ensure that technological development leading to disruption occurs without dampening the potential and most importantly, the career aspirations of current and future generations? Essentials of modern career development include networking, provision for dual careers in couples and mentorship.

DEFINING CSR IN AN ERA OF CORPORATE DISRUPTION

CSR is a strategy that employers use to provide a return on investment not only to shareholders but also to all stakeholders, direct and indirect. External stakeholders include the community, consumers, suppliers, and, most importantly, prospective and current employees (Brammer, Millington, & Rayton, 2007). Increasingly, organisations are conceiving themselves as social enterprises, an umbrella term which encompasses CSR.

An important question is one that poses whether CSR is a trade-off for maximising revenue and profit growth as well as its accountability to assure profitability (Freeman, 1984). The risk for boards is that if an inconsistency between profits and social responsibility occurs, for example, enhanced costs associated with the latter, it will deter attempts to proceed CSR (Hayek, 1969; Karnani, 2011).

These days, given the community's growing attention and investment in the economic and environmental welfare of their people including well-being and a range of other social issues, profit maximisation is not the sole focus of Boards. Additionally, globalisation requires Boards to accommodate a broad range of additional responsibilities (Kolk & van Tulder, 2010; Scherer & Palazzo, 2011) relating to stakeholder concerns (Calabrese & Lancioni, 2008; Freeman, 1984). Incorporating stakeholders' interests into the business strategy contributes to brand enhancement and hence profitability (Carroll & Shabana, 2010), and a proactive approach is more likely to result in reaching higher worth as consumers turn to those companies that do so (Calabrese, 2012; Carroll & Buchholtz, 2009). Furthermore, it is important to launch a pre-emptive CSR strategy so as to gain community confidence (Davis, 1973). Finally, CSR provides opportunities for innovation (Husted & Allen, 2007) and, through focussing on stakeholder needs, leads to competitive advantage (Calabrese & Scoglio, 2012; Kurucz et al., 2008; Porter & Kramer, 2011).

To consider, simultaneously shareholder and stakeholder interests, companies need to keep an eye on their organisational values and interests and the public demonstration of this (Porter & Kramer, 2011). In other words, the stronger and proactive the CSR stance and its alignment with the cultural values of the organisation, the greater the likelihood of profitably as well as social and environmental issues (Maon et al., 2010). There is evidence of an association between poor CSR performance and poor economic/financial performance (Wood, 2010).

Conversely, Boards that create CSR as a core strategy will achieve greater competitive advantage (Nidumolu et al., 2010). For this reason, the strategic role of CSR in creating value in the long term, is important as it is a source of innovation (Husted & Allen, 2007), and competitive advantage (Porter & Kramer, 2011).

It is important to include career as a sustainability initiative of an organisation in its CSR portfolio. Commissioning CSR with the objective of enhancing career pathway requires a fundamental transformation in administrative thinking and simultaneously, the development and implementation of tools for supporting career activities (Porter & Kramer, 2010).

CSR is a long-range plan of action (Falck & Heblich, 2007). The communication outreach to future generations of employees, many of whom are consumers, needs to reflect this.

Appreciating the strategic value of CSR is important from learning to mitigate long-term risks affecting industries and for building a socially responsible career outreach for prospective employers. People evaluate the performance of service organisations (including government and not for profits) who provide for the greater value to their communities. Moreover, customers are willing to reward those organisations by becoming loyal consumers. This intention is extended when organisations are regarded as good employers not only for current generations of employees but also future ones. Corporate-giving needs to leverage its expertise in building careers. Businesses bring specific expertise to addressing work and career-related issues, which, in partnership with universities, schools, governments and non-profits, is potentially highly valuable. The culture of CSR influences both the creation as well as the implementation of a career strategy. On the other hand, such a strategy influences the development of careers for future generations. If today's organisations want to compete in the long term, careers and work are important parts of this.

CORPORATE SOCIAL RESPONSIBILITY

CSR is instructive for business strategy as communities are interested in business impacts, whether it is the environment, employment, the nature of products or services. CSR refers to 'context-specific organisational actions and policies that take into account stakeholders' expectations and the triple bottom line of the economic, social, and environmental performance' (Aguinis & Glavas, 2012, p. 339). Employees are important participants in CSR practices that add value to the returns for their employer (Voegtlin & Greenwood, 2016). CSR are optional actions that the organisation's board or management deem are in the best interests of the wider community in which they reside often focussed on environmental, social, cultural, legal and ethical issues (Aguinis & Glavas, 2012). Employment, unemployment and careers are foremost in people's minds, especially when voting a government in or out. 'Career equity' is something that most people value.

There is very little in the literature about CSR for future generations of employees and safeguarding careers and livelihood for them. And yet, it is well-known that CSR certainly shapes work outcomes for employees in terms of identification, satisfaction and performance more generally (Kim, Song, & Lee, 2016).

CSR practices influence careers both now and in the future (Shen & Benson, 2014). Most employees are unaware of their employer's contribution to CSR (Pomering & Dolnicar, 2009). Employers are challenged by different generations in the workplace today, particularly Generation Y millennials (born from 1981 to 2000), who seem to attract a lot of criticism (Gursoy, Chi, & Karadag, 2013). Generation Y are seeking challenging careers that provide meaning and value (Brown, Thomas, & Bosselman, 2015).

CSR and identifying the right capability are two of the most important issues that employers are tackling today. At a time when people do not have lifetime careers with their employers, the issue for organisational and political leaders is how they think and act responsibly to deliver or protect future career prospects. Achieving this outcome will require a stronger understanding of the link between technical and social systems. Guiding people, especially early career incumbents, into the future, recognising the prospects that surface in their life course and creatively developing options as discussed in this book are required. New challenges will continue to emerge as power and control processes are disrupted. Gaining philosophical and economic insight is equally important

In considering work and career choices, employees evaluate CSR based on brand alignment and priorities (McShane & Cunningham, 2012).

CORPORATE CAREER CITIZENSHIP

Corporate career citizenship potentially takes CSR one step further. It is the process of integrating a sustainable career strategy into organisational goals and strategies in the same way that work, health and safety are incorporated. More importantly, it is an enterprise-wide recognition of the legitimacy and importance of a career in the formulation of business strategy and the integration of career issues, now and in the long term, into the strategic planning process. It is also about balancing the financial benefits in relation to career measures which employers, in the main, are resistant to practices that interfere with profitability. The translation of 'careerism' into the strategic perspective involves the consideration of optimising the profitability and competitiveness of an enterprise – private or government, without compromising the career concerns of today's generations about the future.

The social responsibility of enterprises as well as the career commitment to consider strategic decisions around work and careers is termed corporate career citizenship, including business and human resource systems, and processes that impact careers and employment conditions. Using a Corporate Career Citizenship's perspective of social orientation, the employer, that is, the Board and management, assumes the identity of a design thinker who accepts that it is their responsibility for shaping work and careers for future generations. Corporate design thinking combines entrepreneurialism and strategic thinking. The enterprise becomes a stakeholder in the protection and the conservation of career. CSR, in relation to careers, means that the enterprise accepts the importance of career issues and finds ways to incorporate these issues into their business strategies.

Career stewardship involves assuring that talent is not disposed of without considering re-invention. There are five strategic investment domains for enterprises to become more career orientated for the future: (1) development of competencies related to technology change; (2) career training and employee participation programmes; (3) development of organisational competencies in the area of career management; (4) development of capabilities in the routine-based management systems and procedures at the input, process and output sides; and (5) formulation of career-focussed strategic planning.

A CAREER-FOCUSSED ENTERPRISE

A career enterprise would focus on career thinking consisting of (1) a documented corporate career policy detailing career targets and sustainable development objectives; (2) information related to career life cycle of employees; (3) regular reporting on career sustainability strategy; (4) career design system that involves integration of career goals, policies and responsibilities into employees' roles and used as benchmarks for career design programmes; (5) HRM information related to career practices and performance; (6) proof of building career capabilities, improving employee abilities and problem-solving skills to contribute to career design; (7) creation of a healthy, safe and preserving and beneficial career through employee involvement; (8) information pertaining to lifecycle analysis (assessment); (9) employee involvement in bridging the gap between conventional business processes and career strategies; and (10) information on career standards at home and abroad.

Career Value Chain Management

Career value chain management is the integration of career thinking to include work and role design, talent sourcing and selection, development of employees and all the other HRM processes. Career design implies an understanding of how design decisions affect a current or prospective employee's potential for career transitioning, growth and development. Career cycle assessment analysis is a process that evaluates the career, occupational health and resource-related consequences of a career in all the phases as outlined above. Further, network design refers to accommodating career transitions, exchanges with different types of enterprise, for example, public–private exchanges and university and corporation exchanges.

A Career Strategy

Career management is directly linked to human resources management as the effective utilisation of staffing policies results in the accomplishment of both career and organisational goals. Employers need to integrate a career strategy into their business strategy. Career HRM involves the facilitation of a career vision. It is also understood in relation to career design systems; the formal set of procedures and policies that defines how organisations manage external impacts for itself and its workforce.

Achievement of career excellence is contingent on recruiting and retaining employees who are 'design thinking aware' and knowledgeable and experienced in career management that they are capable of achieving the career goals of the enterprise. Career recruiting that screens the candidates' career commitment and sensitivity to career matters has come to stay. Job descriptions are also being changed to specify the number of career aspects in the process of recruitment (Renwick, Redman, & Maguire, 2008).

Design thinking training is a narrower approach although it ultimately is aimed at raising career consciousness, designing specific job-related and technical training, self-managed training and action-learning networks are the different approaches used in career training (Revill, 2000).

Providing monetary and non-monetary incentives to career performance is basic to implementing career management in organisations. Providing incentives go a long way in motivating the employees to be career-friendly. The enterprise can introduce innovative incentive schemes at the monetary and non-monetary levels.

Devising and implementing employee involvement programmes produces a number of career management outcomes. Employee involvement heightens the accomplishment of career goals. Co-opting employees in the decision-making process, empowering of employees and the formation of design thinking teams are excellent ways of enlisting employee involvement.

Design thinking teams are defined as teams of members committed to solving career problems or implementing career management programmes to improve the career performance record of the firm. Design thinking teams are becoming popular in business organisations as the dynamics of production strategy, competitive pressures and the use of advanced technology demand greater commitment (Jabbour & Santos, 2008). As Beard and Rees (2000, cited by Jabbour & Santos, 2008) report, design thinking teams focus on creating ideas to support organisational learning, to identify conflicts and make decisions in the practice of Career Design. Design thinking teams can constitute an important unit of career HRM.

ORGANISATIONAL LEARNING AND THE DEVELOPMENT OF DESIGN THINKING

An underlying premise of implementing career strategy into organisations and corporate careers is the process of transforming a traditional enterprise into one of an enterprise of career management (Pane et al., 2009). The process of organisational learning is the golden route to practising career management of people or sustainable development or corporate careerism. Organisational learning as a process of construction and internalisation of meanings has to take place for career management to take deep roots in the enterprise. It entails a shift in a person's fundamental understandings and meanings of enterprise's goals which are accomplished in the learning process of deconstructing pre-existing meanings and reconstructing new meanings (Cherrier, Russell, & Fielding, 2012).

The Development of Shared Career Knowledge

Understanding is the process of transforming, reducing, elaborating, storing, recovering and using the sensory input of information and it enables the individual to understand and interpret the career of physical, organisational, social, political, natural, economic and related realms of life.

Shared cognitions make it possible for the members to see and interpret the situation through the same lens and take consensual decisions producing shared patterns of action (Cannon & Salas, 2001). Task-specific knowledge, task-related knowledge, knowledge of teammates, and attitudes and beliefs are the four types of shared knowledge (Cannon & Salas, 2001). Task-specific knowledge is specific procedures, sequences, actions and strategies necessary to perform a task. Task-related knowledge involves general aspects of the task and its related processes, which means that the knowledge pertains to the performance of a number of tasks. Team members' knowledge of other members' strengths, weaknesses and tendencies produce cooperative actions. The shared attitudes and beliefs unite the members and create a common bond (Cannon & Salas, 2001).

Shared learning is the process by which a team develops new knowledge and insights that shape actions (Jimenez & Sanz, 2011). Shared learning involves knowledge development including acquiring, sharing, interpretation, integration and storing it for (Huber, 1991, cited by Jimenez & Sanz, 2011). Creation and development of new knowledge structures emerge from the experience as well as reflective observation, ideation and active experimentation (Kolb, 1984, cited by Murray, 2002). The development of the group and organisational cognition depends on 'unbounded learning' which undergoes further shared learning (Murray, 2002). A good mix of debating the pros and cons in framing perspectives contributes to improving group ideation, problem-solving and outcomes (Mohammad & Dumville, 2001). Active interactions in the group and interpersonal exchanges lead to shared information processing and creation of shared knowledge (Mohammed & Dumville, 2001;

Van den Bossche et al., 2011). Interpretation is contingent on interactions and deliberations and open expositions on issues. Constructive conflict offers the members an opportunity to challenge the views of others and modify and refine contending contents of information (Van den Bossche et al., 2011).

The significance of shared cognition is in relation to the formation and execution of career decisions and the enactment of actions (Zoogah, 2011). Shared learning or shared cognition is the internal cognitive structures that produce action and one can predict team performance from team cognition which suggests that development of shared team knowledge is the key to team action (Cooke et al., 2001). Cognition leads to action and the type of knowledge that people either processes or have stored previously through experience, which, in turn, governs actions. The processing of career knowledge of different forms and the development of shared career cognitions take the enterprise to sustainable activities.

CAREER-FOCUSSED ORGANISATIONAL CULTURE

Each enterprise is differentiated by its own distinguishing culture as an evolved by-product of organisational interaction, which endows an enterprise with a distinctive pattern of action. In relation to career management, career organisational culture is identified to be a key variable (Jabbour & Santos, 2008) and an enterprise's culture and subculture influence and shape the interpretations of and actions around career issues. The literature on culture is ample proof that shared cultural meanings and interpretations provide the enterprise with a platform to launch significant changes, say career management strategies (Howard, 2006).

Career organisational culture is defined as a set of assumptions, values, symbols, and organisational artifacts that reflect either the desire or necessity of a company to operate in a careerly correct way (Jabbour & Santos, 2008). The shared assumptions, beliefs and patterns of thinking are career-like, which is different from a traditional enterprise that does not follow sustainable principles.

Career culture is understood at three levels: the surface level (the adoption of corporate sustainability principles which are visible in technical solutions and sustainability reports), the value level (the adoption of sustainability principles is effected in the employees' value and beliefs on career) and on an underlying level (the adoption of corporate sustainability principles requires a change in core assumptions of career management (Linnenluecke & Griffiths, 2010). In other words, career culture is understood as observable, including the espoused values (strategies, goals and philosophies) and underlying assumptions (unconscious beliefs and perceptions that form the ultimate source of values).

Organisations dominated by openness value organisational processes that facilitate the implementation of ecological principles and ultimately, the enterprise becomes a career-focussed (Linnenluecke & Griffiths, 2010). Further, managers are in a position to influence organisational learning and cultural dynamics and processes by the creation of cross-functional teams, sharing of their 'world vision', reframing of events or stories within the enterprise, development of self-awareness and group awareness and development of procedures to capture and disseminate new knowledge which is pertinent to career management (Bloor, 1999).

Enterprises as rational decision-making entities concentrating on profit maximisation at the cost of careers will be less sustainable in the future. In their management, organisations are moving from techno-centric practices to people-centric ones, and employees will gravitate towards those that support them.

CONCLUSION

The significant and crucial role played by top management in facilitating career management in organisations mediates the impact of public and social interests, regulatory forces and competitive advantage on orientation and career strategies. The senior echelon's knowledge about career risks and problems, their values and aims directly affect corporate career commitment of the organisational participants as these variables directly influence the development of favourable attitudes to careerism (Jabbour & Santos, 2008). The leadership role of the Board and senior managers make a definitive impact in making sustainable practices a core business value (Johnson & Walck, 2004). Further, effective integration of the career dimension into the organisational processes requires the recognition on the part of top leadership that careerism is to be promoted as a new value and that top leadership's commitment that career practices can influence the routines of a company (Jabbour & Santos, 2008).

REFERENCES

Aguinis, H., & Glavas A. (2012). What we know and don't know about corporate social responsibility: A review and research agenda. *Journal of Management*, *38*(4), 932–968.

Bloor, G. (1999). Organisational culture, organisational learning and total quality management: A literature review and synthesis. *Australian Health Review.*, *22*(3), 162–179.

Brammer, S., Millington, A., & Rayton, B. (2007). The contribution of corporate social responsibility to organisational commitment. *International Journal of Human Resource Management*, *18*(10), 1701–1719.

Brown, E. A., Thomas, N. J., & Bosselman, R. H. (2015).
Are they leaving or staying: A qualitative analysis of
turnover issues for Generation Y hospitality employees with
a hospitality education. *International Journal of Hospitality
Management, 46*, 130–137.

Calabrese, A. (2012). Service productivity and service
quality: A necessary trade-off? *International Journal of
Production Economics, 135*(2), 800–812.

Calabrese, A., & Scoglio, F. (2012). Reframing the past: a
new approach in service quality assessment. *Total Quality
Management and Business Excellence, 23* (11–12), 1329–1343.

Calabrese, A., & Lancioni, F. (2008). Analysis of corporate
social responsibility in the service sector: does exist a strategic
path? *Knowledge and Process Management, 15* (2), 107–125.

Cannon, B. J. A., & Salas, E. (2001). Reflections on Shared
Cognition. *Journal of Organisational Behavior, 22*(2), 195–202.

Carroll, A. B., & Buchholtz, A. K. (2009). *Business and
Society: Ethics and Stakeholder Management, 7th Edition.*
Mason, OH: South-Western Cengage Learning.

Carroll A. B., & Shabana, K. M. (2010). The Business Case
for Corporate Social Responsibility: A Review of Concepts,
Research and Practice. *International Journal of Management
Reviews, 12* (1), 85–105.

Cherrier, H., Russell, S. V., & Fielding, K. (2012). Corporate
environmentalism and top management identity negotiation.
Journal of Organisational Change Management, 25(4),
518–534.

Cooke, N. J., Kiekel, P. A., & Helm, E. E. (2001),. Measuring
Team Knowledge During Skill Acquisition of a Complex Task.
International Journal of Cognitive Ergonomics, 5(3), 297–315.

Davis K. (1973). The case for and against business assumption of social responsibilities. *Academy of Management Journal, 16*(2), 312–322.

Gursoy, D., Chi, C. G., & Karadag, E. (2013). Generational differences in work values and attitudes among frontline and service contact employees. *International Journal of Hospitality Management, 32*, 40–48.

Hall, D. T., & Mirvis, P. H. (1995). The new career contract: Developing the whole person at midlife and beyond. *Journal of Vocational Behaviour, 47*(3), 269–289.

Hayek, F. A. (1969). The corporation in a democratic society: in whose interest ought it and will it be run? In H. Ansoff, (Ed.). *Business Strategy*, Harmondsworth: Penguin Books.

Husted. B. W., & Allen, D. B. (2007). Strategic Corporate Social Responsibility and Value Creation among Large Firms: Lessons from the Spanish Experience. *Long Range Planning, 40*, 594–610.

Jabbour, C., & Santos, F. (2008). The central role of human resource management in the search for sustainable organizations. *The International Journal of Human Resource Management, 19*(12), 2133–2154.

Jimenez-Jimenez, D., & Sanz-Valle, R. (2011). Innovation, Organizational Learning, and Performance, *Journal of Business Research, 64*(4), 408–417.

Kolb, D. A. (1984). *Experiential learning: Experience as the source of learning and development.* Newark, NJ: Prentice Hall.

Kolk, A., & van Tulder, R. (2010). International business, corporate social responsibility and sustainable development. *International Business Review, 19*, 119–125.

Kurucz, E., Colbert B., & Wheeler, D. (2008). The business case for corporate social responsibility. In A. Crane, A. McWilliams, D. Matten, J. Moon, & D. Siegel, (Eds.), *The Oxford Handbook of Corporate Social Responsibility* (pp. 83–112).. Oxford: Oxford University Press.

Linnenluecke, M., & Griffiths, A. (2010). Beyond adaptation: Resilience for business in light of climate change and weather extremes. *Business & Society*, *49*(3), 477–511.

Maon, F., Lindgreen A. & Swaen, V. (2010). Organisational Stages and Cultural Phases: A Critical Review and a Consolidative Model of Corporate Social Responsibility Development. *International Journal of Management Reviews*, *12*(1), 20–35.

McShane, L., & Cunningham, P. (2012). To thine own self be true? Employees' judgments of the authenticity of their organisation's corporate social responsibility program. *Journal of Business Ethics*, *108*(1), 81–100.

Mohammed, S., & Dumville, B. C. (2001). Team mental models in a team knowledge framework: Expanding theory and measurement across disciplinary boundaries. *Journal of Organizational Action*, *22*(2), 89–106.

Murray, P. (2002). Cycles of organizational learning: A conceptual approach. *Management Decision*, *40*(3), 239–247.

Nidumolu, R., Prahalad, C. K. & Rangaswami, M. R. (2009). Why sustainability is now the key driver of innovation. *Harvard Business Review*, *87*(9), 25–34.

Pane Haden, S. S., Oyler, J. D., & Humphreys, J. H. (2009). Historical, Practical, and Theoretical Perspectives on Green Management: An Exploratory Analysis. *Management Decision*, *47*(7), 1041–1055.

Porter M. E, & Kramer M. R. (2011). Creating Shared Value. *Harvard Business Review, 89*(1–2), 62–77.

Pomering, A., & Dolnicar, S. (2009). Assessing the prerequisite of successful CSR implementation: Are consumers aware of CSR initiatives? *Journal of Business Ethics, 85*(2s), 285–301.

Renwick, D., Redman, T., & Maguire, S. (2008). Career HRM: A review, process model, and research agenda. *University of Sheffield Management School Discussion Paper Series, 1,* 1–46.

Revill, C. (2000). The careering of personnel/human resource management: An assessment. *International Journal of Applied HRM, 1*(3), 1–30.

Shen, J., & Benson, J. (2014). When CSR is a social norm how socially responsible human resource management affects employee work behaviour. *Journal of Management, 42*(6), 1723–1746.

Van den Bossche, P., Gijselaers, W. et al. (2011). Team Learning: Building Shared Mental Models, *Instructional Science, 39*(3), 283–301.

Voegtlin, C., & Greenwood, M. (2016). Corporate social responsibility and human resource management: A systematic review and conceptual analysis. *Human Resource Management Review, 26*(3), 181–197.

Wood, D. J. (2010). Measuring Corporate Social Performance: A Review. *International Journal of Management Reviews, 12*(1), 50–84.

Zoogah, D. B. (2011). The dynamics of career HRM actions: A cognitive social information processing approach. *German Journal of Human Resource Management, 25*(2), 117–139.

INDEX